The
Berlin
Wall
Story

Biography of a Monument

Ch. Links Verlag

The Author

Hans-Hermann Hertle, PhD, born in Eisern/Siegen in 1955, senior research fellow at the Centre for Contemporary History Potsdam. Numerous books on social and contemporary history and documentaries, including: "When the Wall came tumbling down", ARD television documentary, 1999 (with Gunther Scholz); "Damals in der DDR. Der Alltag im Arbeiter- und Bauernstaat", 2004 (with Stefan Wolle); "Chronik des Mauerfalls", 12th edition, 2009.

The German National Library catalogs this publication in the German National Bibliography; detailed bibliographical information available online at: www.dnb.de.

2nd edition, updated, Berlin, May 2016
© Christoph Links Verlag GmbH, 2011
Schönhauser Allee 36, 10435 Berlin, Tel.: + 49-30-44 02 32-0
www.christoph-links-verlag.de; mail@christoph-links-verlag.de
Translation: Timothy Jones; legends: Katy Derbyshire
Art direction and graphic design: Leitwerk. Büro für Kommunikation, Cologne, www.leitwerk.com
Cover design: KahaneDesign, Berlin; cover photo: Paul Glaser, Berlin (East German border guards observate a police action in West Berlin, Potsdamer Platz 1988)
Printed by: Graspo CZ
ISBN 978-3-86153-650-5

Contents

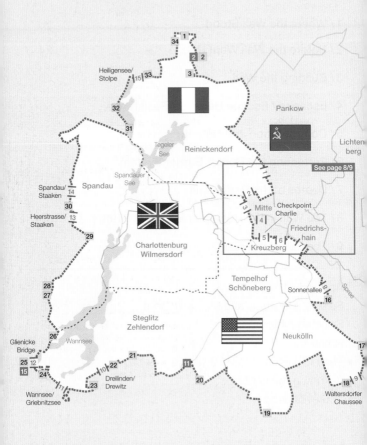

Heiligensee/
Stolpe

Pankow

Tegeler
See

Reinickendorf

Lichten-
berg

Spandauer
See

Spandau

See page 8/9

Spandau/
Staaken

Heerstrasse/
Staaken

Mitte

Checkpoint
Charlie

Friedrichs-
hain

Kreuzberg

Charlottenburg
Wilmersdorf

Tempelhof
Schöneberg

Sonnenallee

Steglitz
Zehlendorf

Neukölln

Glienicke
Bridge

Wannsee

Spree

Dreilinden/
Drewitz

Wannsee/
Griebnitzsee

Waltersdorfer
Chaussee

6

The Berlin Wall

Border Crossings

| 8 | Sonnenallee: West Berliners, FRG citizens
| 9 | Waltersdorfer Chaussee: West Berliners, transit travellers by air

Vehicular and railway traffic to and from West Berlin goes over the border crossings
| 10 | Dreilinden/Drewitz (motorway)
| 11 | Wannsee/Griebnitzsee (railway)
| 12 | Glienicke Bridge: Allied military personell and since 1985 diplomats
| 13 | Heerstrasse / Staaken (major road, until 1987)
| 14 | Spandau / Staaken (railway)
| 15 | Heiligensee / Stolpe (motorway, from 1982)

For border crossings | 1 | – | 7 | see following page.

Remnants of the Wall

1 Bergfelde
2 Glienicke Nordbahn
3 Entenschnabel
16 Neukölln/Sonnenallee
17 Rudow
18 Schönefeld
19 Mahlow
20 Teltow
21 Kleinmachnow
22 Drewitz border crossing
23 Dreilinden
24 Griebnitzsee
25 Glienicke Bridge
26 Sacrow and Kladow
27 Gross Glienicke
28 Gross Glienicke "Wall cemetery"
29 Weinbergshöhe
30 Staaken
31 Spandau
32 Niederneuendorf
33 Stolpe-Süd
34 Hohen Neuendorf

For remnants 4 – 15 see following page.

See pictures of remnants of the Wall one can still find today:
www.chronik-der-mauer.de/remnants

Photographs of the Wall and death strip then and now (See chapter 1)

2 Between Frohnau and Bieselheide
11 Teltow-Seehof
15 Glienicke Bridge

See more pictures of how the death strip has changed since the Wall fell:
www.chronik-der-mauer.de/thenandnow

Marzahn
Hellersdorf

Treptow
Köpenick

Border Crossings

| 1 | Bornholmer Strasse: West Berliners, FRG citizens, GDR citizens, diplomats
| 2 | Chausseestrasse: West Berliners, GDR citizens
| 3 | Invalidenstrasse: West Berliners, GDR citizens
| 4 | Friedrichstrasse Railway Station: West Berliners, FRG citizens, GDR citizens, diplomats, foreigners, Allied military personnel
| 5 | "Checkpoint Charlie" Friedrichstrasse / Zimmerstrasse: Allied military personnel, foreigners, diplomats, GDR citizens
| 6 | Heinrich-Heine-Strasse: FRG citizens, GDR citizens, diplomats
| 7 | Oberbaum Bridge: West Berliners, FRG citizens

For border crossings | 8 | – | 15 | see previous page.

Remnants of the Wall

- 4 Bornholmer Strasse
- 5 Bernauer Strasse
- 6 Nordbahnhof
- 7 Invalidenfriedhof
- 8 Reichstag/Brandenburg Gate
- 9 Potsdamer Platz
- 10 Gropiusbau
- 11 "Checkpoint Charlie" border crossing
- 12 Kommandantenstrasse
- 13 Schillingbrücke
- 14 East Side Gallery
- 15 Treptow/Schlesischer Busch

For remnants 1 – 3 and 16 – 34 see previous page.

See pictures of remnants of the Wall one can still find today:
www.chronik-der-mauer.de/remnants

Photographs of the Wall and death strip then and now (See chapter 1)

- 4 Bornholmer Strasse border crossing
- 6 Reichstag
- 7 Gropiusbau
- C "Checkpoint Charlie" Friedrich-/Zimmerstrasse

See more pictures of how the death strip has changed since the Wall fell:
www.chronik-der-mauer.de/thenandnow

Friedrichshain

...zmarktstr.

13
East Side Gallery
14 Mühlenstr.
Warschauer Str.

Oberbaum-brücke 7

Skalitzer Str.

Hauptstr.

15

Spree

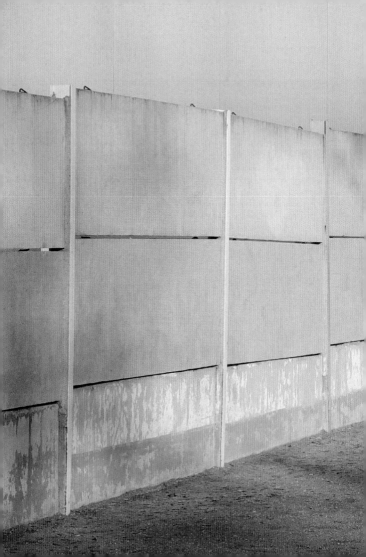

1
Where the Wall Stood

6 At the Reichstag building, Berlin-Mitte, 2005. < West / East >
Previous page: Berlin Wall Memorial, Bernauer Strasse.

Then and Now

1,084 photos taken by the East German border troops in the 1980s provide a complete topography of the wall. Fifteen years after the wall was torn down, Dajana Marquardt returned to the places where the military took the photos, and took comparative shots.

You can view all the pictures at: www.chronik-der-mauer.de/thenandnow

6 At the Reichstag building, Berlin-Mitte, 1980s. < West / East >

7 Gropiusbau and House of Ministries (now Federal Ministry of Finance), Berlin-Mitte, 2005.
< West / East >

7 Gropiusbau and House of Ministries (now Federal Ministry of Finance), Berlin-Mitte, 1980s.
< West / East >

15 Glienicke Bridge, Potsdam, 2005. Coming from Potsdam, East Germany, heading for West Berlin.

15 Glienicke Bridge, Potsdam, 1980s. Coming from Potsdam, East Germany, heading for West Berlin.

11 Teltow-Seehof, 2005. < West/ East >

11 Teltow-Seehof, 1980s. < West/ East >

2 Between Frohnau and Bieselheide, Glienicke / Nordbahn, 2005. < West/ East >

2 Between Frohnau and Bieselheide, Glienicke / Nordbahn, 1980s. < West/ East >

4 Bornholmer Strasse, Böse Bridge, 2005. < East / West >

4 Bornholmer Strasse, Böse Bridge, 1980s. < East / West >

C Checkpoint Charlie, 2007. Coming from West Berlin, heading for East Berlin.

C Checkpoint Charlie, 1970s. Coming from West Berlin, heading for East Berlin.

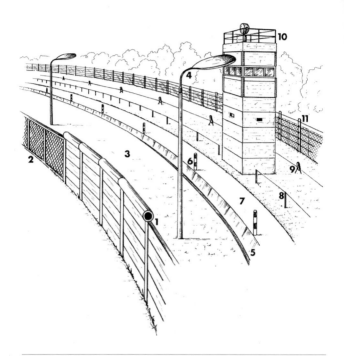

The Wall and the death strip (1970s)

1 Concrete flagstone wall
  with or without piping on top
2 Wire mesh fencing
3 Inspection track
4 Lighting
5 Anti-vehicle trench

6 Outer limit of border patrol track
7 Patrol track
8 Guide wire of guard dog track
9 Alarm
10 Observation tower
11 Fencing with built-in alarm

Berlin Wall Statistics

Total length of 156.4 km

43.7 km through Berlin

112.7 km around the outskirts

including

63.8 km through built-up areas

32.0 km through woods

22.7 km through open terrain

38.0 km water border
(rivers and lakes)

41.9 km "Border Wall 75"
(height 3.60 m)

59.0 km border wall made of
prefabricated concrete slabs

68.4 km wire mesh fencing
as first barrier

161.0 km illuminated strip

113.9 km alarm fencing

186 watchtowers

31 command towers

484 guard dogs

Based on information from GDR border troops (1989)

Between 1961 and 1989 the West Berlin police registered:

at least 5,075 successful escapes through the Wall and death strip,
including 574 desertions

1,709 cases in which border guards used firearms,
with at least 119 escapees injured

456 bullet impacts in West Berlin;
West Berlin police returned fire in 14 cases

37 bomb attacks on the Wall

Recent investigations have certified
at least 138 deaths at the Berlin Wall.

2
Before the Wall
Went Up

Germany in 1945: The end of the war and occupation

When the Wall is built in Berlin in 1961, Germany has already been a divided country for sixteen years.

At least 55 million people, including 25 million civilians, died as a result of the war and the crimes of the Nazi regime. The defeat that put an end to the Nazi dictatorship in May 1945 was therefore also a liberation.

In 1945, the German Reich is occupied by the Allies and divided into a Soviet, an American, a British and a French zone. Berlin, to that date the capital, is also divided up into four sectors.

The Four Powers determine the new political, economic and social orders in their respective zones. Their major objectives are demilitarisation, de-Nazification and democratisation. At the Potsdam Conference in the summer of 1945, however, it is also decided that the economic unity of Germany is to be preserved and that its political reunification is soon to follow.

But the anti-Hitler coalition soon splits up. The Soviet Union extends the power bases it has gained during the war by means of force. In the Central European countries, it sets up new dictatorships under the communist parties it controls.

The USA leaves troops in Europe and Asia to stem the Soviet Union's imperialist power politics. It guarantees its support to all free peoples threatened by communism.

< Previous page: Soldiers raising the Soviet flag on top of the Reichstag building in Berlin, May 1945.

The Cold War begins.
Two irreconcilable ideologies
struggle for global power
and influence.
And one main arena
of this Cold War
is the divided Germany.

Stalin (Soviet Union) – Truman (USA) – Churchill (Great Britain): "The Big Three" in Potsdam, July 1945.

At the Yalta Conference in February 1945, the heads of the United States, the Soviet Union and Britain decide to divide up Germany. In the final phase of World War II, the US President Franklin Roosevelt, the Soviet Communist Party General Secretary Joseph Stalin and the British Prime Minister Winston Churchill agree to form four occupation zones with a joint Allied Control Council. Berlin is also divided into four "sectors". France, which does not have a representative in Yalta, is given its own zone and its own sector of Berlin. The follow-up conference in Potsdam in July and August 1945 outlines the goals of the occupation policy in Germany: democratisation, denazification, demilitarisation and decartelisation. However, the Allies have very different ideas about how to achieve these goals. The anti-Hitler coalition collapses soon after the end of the war. The divided post-war Germany and the divided capital city of Berlin become one of the main arenas of the Cold War.

The founding of two German states in 1949

In the three western zones and the western sectors of Berlin, the occupying powers of the USA, Great Britain and France prescribe a form of democracy on the western model for the West Germans and West Berliners. In 1949, a democratic constitutional state with a multiparty system, separation of powers, pluralistic institutions and free elections is set up on the basis of a system of private enterprise and ownership: the Federal Republic of Germany (FRG) – a bulwark against communism.

In the Soviet occupation zone and in the Soviet sector of Berlin, a communist one-party system on the basis of a state-run economy is established under Soviet control. The sole ruling Socialist Unity Party (SED) brings the bourgeois parties and unions into line and suppresses any political opposition. Free elections are not held. On 7 October 1949, the "German Democratic Republic" (GDR) is proclaimed on the territory of the Soviet occupation zone – a military outpost of the Soviet Union in Central Europe.

After the two states have been founded, the West German government claims to be the sole representative of all Germans; it does not recognise the GDR as a state, since the GDR government has not been chosen in free elections. If other states enter into diplomatic relations with the GDR, the West German government reacts with countermeasures, sometimes even breaking off diplomatic ties. In this way, West Germany succeeds in politically isolating the GDR until the end of the 1960s.

The GDR itself at first also has the objective of German unity, but only under a socialist flag: the SED rulers reject reunification by means of a free, universal and equal vote.

Rebuilding in the GDR is hampered by the fact that the Soviet Union seizes large amounts of industrial equipment and demands high war reparations. The socialist planned economy turns out to be inefficient. The economic gap between the GDR and West Germany becomes deeper and deeper in the 1950s. Many residents of East Germany decide to flee for financial, political and family reasons.

"From Stettin in the Baltic to Trieste in the Adriatic, an iron curtain has descended across the Continent."

"Warsaw, Berlin, Prague, Vienna, Budapest, Belgrade, Bucharest and Sofia, all these famous cities and the populations around them lie in what I must call the Soviet sphere, and all are subject in one form or another, not only to Soviet influence but to a very high and, in many cases, increasing measure of control from Moscow."

Winston Churchill in Fulton, USA, 5 March 1946.

Escape from the GDR

Between 1945 and 1961, three and a half million people flee from the Soviet occupation zone and the later GDR to West Germany. They flee because they have relatives in the West, because their property has been taken away from them, because they are discriminated against and persecuted as Christians, because the supply of food and other commodities is deficient, and because political freedom is dying.

SED resolutions on speeding up the establishment of socialism, pension cuts, increased prices for food and finally the raising of the stipulated work rates trigger the national uprising of 17 June 1953, which culminates in demands for free elections and reunification. Soviet soldiers and tanks rush to the aid of the SED regime and put down the rebellion. After 17 June 1953, the number of people fleeing the GDR increases dramatically; in the ensuing years, it swells again with every repressive measure and every political event that deepens the division of Germany: in 1955 after the signing of the Warsaw Pact; in 1957 when the campaign against the churches intensifies; in 1960 with the forced collectivisation of agriculture.

The SED's reaction to people's "voting with their feet" grows increasingly harsh: as early as 26 May 1952, military units block off the border to West Germany with barbed wire. At the same time, many streets between East and West Berlin and direct telephone communications are cut off. Because of the Allied status of the city, traffic continues to run via the remaining 81 sector crossing points despite the economic and political division – and the escapes via East Berlin to West Berlin continue too.

In December 1957, the SED leadership tightens the penal law: leaving the GDR is prosecuted as "illegal emigration" ("Republikflucht") and punished by up to three years' imprisonment; even preparing and attempting such an escape carries a prison sentence.

See also: www.chronik-der-mauer.de > English > 1961 > April/May

In the summer of 1961 the stream of refugees through Berlin swells dramatically. GDR propaganda accuses the West of wooing people away and of human trafficking. But the East German leadership really knows the true motives for fleeing the country: rejection of the political developments in the GDR and better chances of survival in the West.

East German refugees at the Marienfelde Refugee Center in West Berlin, August 1961.

24-year-old machine fitter from Thuringia, single, 14 July 1961
"I told some members of the Soviet occupation force that they should go home and take Ulbricht with them. Someone from the SED heard me say it and threatened that soon I wouldn't have the chance to say things like that in public. So I preferred to disappear from the Zone."

35-year-old tractor driver from the Anklam district, married, with children, 18 July 1961 "I couldn't bear the pressure put on me to join the SED and Combat Group any more. The bad pay on the collective farm and the poor food supply also had something to do with it. And I also thought about bringing up my children; I try to raise them in the Christian faith. And the school and kindergarten made that almost impossible."

Refugee movement from the GDR and the eastern sector of Berlin 1949–1961

Year	People	Young people under 25
1949	129,245	–
1950	197,788	–
1951	165,648	–
1952	182,393	–
1953	331,390	48.7 %
1954	184,198	49.1 %
1955	252,870	49.1 %
1956	279,189	49.0 %
1957	261,622	52.2 %
1958	204,092	48.2 %
1959	143,917	48.3 %
1960	199,188	48.8 %
1961*	207,026	49.2 %

* until 13 August 1961, the day the Wall was built.

"The GDR, Germany, is the country where it must be determined that Marxism-Leninism is right, and that communism is the higher, better social order for industrial nations as well. [...] If socialism does not prevail in the GDR, if communism does not show itself to be superior and viable here, then we have not won."

Anastas Mikoyan, Soviet First Deputy Premier, June 1961.

Nikita Khrushchev and Walter Ulbricht at the Fifth Socialist Unity Party Congress in East Berlin, July 1958 ("Socialism is victorious").

The Khrushchev ultimatum and the Berlin crisis 1958 – 1961

The Soviet Union sees free West Berlin as a "splinter" that must be removed from the heart of "socialist Europe".

On 27 November 1958, the Soviet communist party and state leader Nikita Khrushchev issues an ultimatum: if the Western Powers do not enter into negotiations on a peace accord and the transformation of West Berlin into a "free city" within six months, the Soviet Union will sign a unilateral peace agreement with the GDR, in which it hands over all Soviet rights and responsibilities with regard to Berlin to the GDR government – in particular, the control over the connecting routes to West Germany by land, water and air.

The ultimatum is tantamount to revoking the four-power status of Berlin, driving the Western Powers from West Berlin – and preventing people from fleeing. But the United States, Great Britain and France do not give in to the pressure. To the disappointment of the SED leadership, Khrushchev postpones his ultimatum several times. The Soviet leader seems to shrink back from the announced confrontation and its incalculable consequences, which include the risk of an atomic war with the United States.

Nikita Khrushchev and John F. Kennedy in Vienna, 3 June 1961.

In the spring of 1961, the economic situation in the GDR rapidly goes downhill, the problems with supply increase – and the stream of refugees grows. The GDR faces an imminent economic and political collapse. Ulbricht presses for radical measures; Khrushchev, however, continues to call for restraint. He says that no decisions should be taken before his summit meeting with the American president John F. Kennedy on 3 and 4 June 1961 in Vienna. The Soviet-US summit is a frosty affair. Khrushchev repeats his ultimatum, setting a new deadline for the end of 1961. Kennedy rejects the ultimatum and warns of a "cold winter" to come. Even war is mentioned. The American president reacts firmly to the threats: he announces a massive rise in defence spending and the despatch of six more US divisions to Europe. This, and the acute threat to the existence of the GDR in the summer of 1961, causes Khrushchev to step back from his ultimate goals and to agree instead to sealing off the sector border in Berlin.

In July 1961, in the greatest secrecy, the SED leadership begins with concrete military and technical preparations for closing off the border. By the evening of 12 August 1961, fewer than one hundred officials from the party, state and military apparatus have been let in on the plans.

See also: www.chronik-der-mauer.de > English > 1961 > June > 4

Nikita Khrushchev to Hans Kroll, West German Ambassador in Moscow, November 1961 "There were only two sorts of countermeasure: an air transport blockade or the Wall. The former would have involved us in a serious conflict with the United States that might have led to war. That is something I could not and did not want to risk. So that left the Wall. And I do not want to conceal the fact from you that I was the person who in the end gave the order to build it."

SED chairman Walter Ulbricht at an international press conference in the large hall of the House of Ministries in East Berlin, 15 June 1961.

"No one has the intention of building a wall."

Walter Ulbricht at an international press conference in East Berlin, 15 June 1961.

International press conference in East Berlin, 15 June 1961
Annamarie Doherr (Reporter, Frankfurter Rundschau) "I would like to ask an additional question: Mr Chairperson, does the building of a free city imply in your opinion that there will be a state border erected at the Brandenburg Gate, and are you ready to assume the full responsibility of the consequences of such a decision?"

Walter Ulbricht (Chairman of the State Council of the German Democratic Republic) "I understand your question that you are saying that there are people in West Germany who want us to mobilise the construction workers of the Capital of the GDR in order to build a wall, isn't it? To my knowledge, there are no such intentions, because the construction workers in the Capital of the GDR are more than busy with building houses and their manpower is fully needed for this task. No one has the intention of building a wall."

3
Building the Wall

Building the Wall

During the night preceding Sunday, 13 August 1961, SED leader Walter Ulbricht gives the order to seal off the zone border. Erich Honecker, a member of the politburo, is in charge of the operation. It is hoped that the people will be distracted over the weekend.

More than 10,000 armed personnel from the People's Police and the border police, assisted by several thousand Combat Group members, rip up streets in the middle of Berlin, pile up pieces of asphalt and paving stones to form barricades, drive concrete posts into the ground and erect barbed-wire barriers. They seal off all sector crossing points with the exception of 13.

Through traffic by overground and underground rail is permanently cut off, inter-sector traffic is reduced to one train and one underground platform in Friedrichstrasse railway station and 13 of the 33 stations in East Berlin are shut down.

The National People's Army is on standby with more than 7,000 soldiers and several hundred tanks, ready to prevent anyone from breaking through the sector borders. Soviet troops deployed around Berlin form a third line of security.

The West Berliners stand on one side of the barbed wire and the East Berliners and people living outside the city limits on the other, all of them stunned by events. The bystanders on the eastern side are held in check with machine guns by Combat Groups and People's Police; anyone who protests is arrested. On the western side, the West Berlin police guard the border barriers against distraught citizens.

< Previous page: West Berliners by the Wall between Kreuzberg and Berlin-Mitte, late August 1961.

East Berliners by the barbed wire, 13 August 1961.

Combat Groups sealing off the Brandenburg Gate, 14 August 1961.

Soviet-made East German army tanks (T-34) advancing towards Warschauer Bridge on 13 August 1961.

"On 13 August I saw tears in the eyes of men whom I had never seen cry before. The blow was hard and terrible. The reaction was not the awakening of any immediate will to resist, but sheer depression."

A doctor from East Berlin who fled on 14 August 1961.

Decision by the GDR Council of Ministers, 12 August 1961 "To put a stop to the hostile activities of the revanchist and militarist forces of West Germany and West Berlin, a control system is being introduced on the border of the GDR, including the border to the western sectors of Greater Berlin, as is the case on the borders of every sovereign state. Reliable surveillance and effective control must be ensured on the West Berlin borders to curb subversive activities. As of now, these borders may only be crossed by GDR citizens with special permission."

Communiqué issued by the Senate of Berlin, 13 August 1961 "The Berlin Senate condemns the unlawful and inhuman measures taken by the splitters of Germany, the oppressors of East Berlin and the menacers from West Berlin. Sealing off the Zone and the Soviet sector from West Berlin means that the barrier of a concentration camp has been set up through the middle of Berlin. The Senate and the people of Berlin expect the Western Powers to take decisive steps with regard to the Soviet government."

Pierre Messmer, French Defence Minister in 1961 "The question was very simple: was it advisable to oppose the building of the Wall with force? The answer was negative. I think it would have been technically possible. But I doubt that we would have been able to maintain such a position politically."

Henry Kissinger, Advisor to the US National Security Council in 1961 "The problem was that it was all very well to make nuclear threats until you examine what the consequences will be. And it was very difficult to come up with contingency plans in which there was a rational outcome that was foreseeable. You could make a plan for a military move on the Autobahn but you would very quickly reach the limit of your capabilities and then you would have the onus and the responsibility for escalation."

15 August 1961: Conrad Schumann is the first East German border guard who escapes to the West. More than 2,500 East German border guards and soldiers escape the country between the construction and the fall of the wall.

15 August 1961: Jump to freedom

The 19-year-old Conrad Schumann, a member of the Border Police, is a trained shepherd and comes from Zschochau in Saxony. In the early hours of 12 August 1961, his brigade is transferred from Dresden to the Berlin sector border. His salary is increased by 30 East German marks in "danger money" to a total of 370 marks.

On the afternoon of 15 August 1961, he becomes the first East German border guard to escape to the West, bravely jumping over the barbed-wire barrier at the corner of Bernauer and Ruppiner Strasse. The photograph goes around the world, bearing with it the message: the GDR's own troops are running away.

Schumann later related that his escape had been strongly motivated by the following experience: "As a border policeman, I saw how a small girl who was visiting her grandmother in East Berlin was held back by the border soldiers and not allowed to cross into West Berlin. Even though her parents were waiting only a few metres from the barbed-wire barriers that had already been laid out, the girl was simply sent back to East Berlin." Conrad Schumann never thought of himself as a hero. In 1998 he took his own life owing to personal problems.

The barbed wire does not stop people from trying to escape. In the night of 17 to 18 August 1961, construction squads begin replacing the barbed-wire barriers with a breeze-block wall.

Lothar Wesner, bricklayer in 1961 "We were taken to Friedrichstrasse/ Zimmerstrasse and then we began to lay bricks under supervision. It was all so confusing. I had the feeling that I was contributing to not being able to see my own relatives. And that was depressing and painful."

Willy Brandt, 16 August 1961 "Our compatriots behind the barbed wire, behind the cement posts and behind the tanks; our compatriots in the Zone, who today are being watched over by the troops of the Red Army so that they cannot show what they want; at this hour today, our compatriots are looking towards us. We know what hate, what bitterness, what desperation is in their hearts today and during these days. We know that only the tanks are preventing them from giving free rein to their outrage. [...]"

"Today I wrote a personal letter to the President of the United States of America, John Kennedy. And in all frankness I told him my opinion: Berlin expects more than words – Berlin expects political action."

16 August 1961: Willy Brandt, West Berlin mayor, at a demonstration by 200,000 West Berliners at Schöneberg Town Hall.

John F. Kennedy, letter to Willy Brandt, 18 August 1961 "Since it represents a resounding confession of failure and of political weakness, this brutal border closing evidently represents a basic Soviet decision which only war could reverse. Neither you nor we, nor any of our Allies, have ever supposed that we should go to war on this point."

John F. Kennedy, letter to Lyndon B. Johnson, 18 August 1961
"Dear Mr. Vice President, I greatly appreciate your having taken on this mission in Germany and West Berlin on short notice. Your primary objective is to put the people of West Berlin at ease as well as to have a candid talk with Mayor Willy Brandt to try to make him see that it will be very important in the coming months to avoid hasty criticism of others.
Sincerely yours, John F. Kennedy"

Lyndon B. Johnson, 19 August 1961 "I have come across the ocean to Berlin by direction of the President of the United States, John F. Kennedy. He wants you to know and I want you to know, the United States wants you to know, that the commitment we have given to the freedom of West Berlin and to the rights of western access to Berlin is firm. To the people of East Berlin I would say: Do not lose courage and confidence. While tyrannies may seem for the moment to proceed for ever, their days are numbered."

Lyndon B. Johnson, Memorandum to John F. Kennedy, 21 August 1961 "No one who saw our troops arriving and the welcome they were given could ever forget that scene. Our heavy artillery brought the greatest cheering of all. At this time, it is impossible to say with all certainty how long West Berlin's reinforced morale will hold.

But at least we are now in a position to influence the course of events, and to do so in a way that will pose difficulties for Communist expansion."

Parade of six US Army motorised convoys with troop reinforcements, some 1,500 men, in West Berlin, 20 August 1961.

24 August 1961: Günter Litfin – the first escapee to be shot dead

On 22 August 1961, the SED politburo decides to instruct the People's Police and the People's Army that anyone "violating the laws of our GDR is to be called to order, if necessary by use of weapons."

On 24 August 1961, the first escapee is shot dead: Günter Litfin worked as a tailor in West Berlin until 13 August. On the afternoon of 24 August, he tries to escape near the Reichstag building. When he is spotted, he takes the shortest route: at Humboldt harbour, he jumps into the canal separating East and West Berlin and swims strongly towards West Berlin. He has almost reached the safe haven of the western bank when a border guard with a submachine gun fires a round at the unarmed and defenceless swimmer.

Günter Litfin is hit in the head and sinks underwater. His dead body is pulled out of the water in the early evening.

See also: www.chronik-der-mauer.de/victims/guenter-litfin

On 23 August 1961 the number of sector crossing points is reduced to seven. From this day on, West Berliners need a pass to visit East Berlin. But from 23 August 1961, this pass is no longer available, because the GDR issuing offices at the West Berlin train stations Zoo and Westkreuz have been shut on the order of the Western Allies in agreement with the Senate. This means that West Berliners are not able to visit East Berlin until the first agreement on passes is signed in 1963.

Pictures left and above: A long farewell, September 1961.

"In the entire area near the national border [...], every form of contact, waving, the exchange of greetings or letters and the handing over of presents etc. [...] is to be prevented."

Order of the East Berlin Chief of Police, 28 August 1961.

8 September 1961: An East-West wedding

An East-West wedding three weeks after the construction of the Wall. The apartment house in Bernauer Strasse belongs to the east part of Berlin; the pavement is in the west part. The door of the house is walled up on the inside; the lowest apartment has already been vacated. The mother of Monika Schaar, family members and neighbours lower their wedding bouquets on ropes.

"First we stood at my mother's window, then we drove home to my parents-in-law. Of course we often thought of my mother, but we couldn't change the situation."

Monika Schaar, a bride in 1961.

Monika Schaar's mother looking down to her daughter.

Monika Schaar, the bride, in front of her mother's house.

Bernauer Strasse 25: Escaping from the first floor. 77-year-old Frieda Schulze, 24 September 1961.

20 September 1961: Evacuating houses on the border

In the streets of East Berlin and the environs of Berlin where the sector border runs alongside houses, many people use the opportunity to jump or lower themselves on ropes from their apartments to get to the West.

For this reason, the order is given on 20 September to evict and relocate tenants from all apartments offering good chances of escape. In Bernauer Strasse, some residents are still able to escape to West Berlin territory by jumping from the windows of their apartments. 77-year-old Frieda Schulze is held back by members of the Combat Groups. But West Berliners climb up onto a window ledge of her house and free her so that she can fall into a jumping sheet provided by the West Berlin fire brigade.

For 80-year-old Olga Segler from Bernauer Strasse 34, the leap ends in her death. She dies the next day from the internal injuries she suffered while jumping.

After the house is evacuated, the windows are walled up and barbed-wire barriers placed on the roofs.

Man behind barbed wire, Bernauer Strasse, 4 September 1961.

US tanks at Checkpoint Charlie, 25/26 October 1961.

27/28 October 1961: Tank standoff at Checkpoint Charlie

US tanks equipped with shovels drive up to Checkpoint Charlie on 25 October 1961. General Lucius Clay, the personal representative of US President Kennedy in Berlin, wants to demonstrate that the Americans will not allow their right to drive anywhere in Berlin to be taken away from them. The escalation is the result of an order issued by the GDR Interior Ministry on 23 October. It stipulates that US soldiers in civilian clothes should identify themselves to East German checkpoint personnel when driving into East Berlin. The US military sees this as an attack on their rights as Allies.

On 27 October, the Soviet Union reacts to the challenge and in its turn deploys tanks at Checkpoint Charlie. For sixteen hours, American and Soviet tanks face off in Friedrichstrasse.

5 December 1961: "Last train to freedom"

Train driver Harry Deterling and his wife Ingrid do not want to live in the GDR as prisoners with their four children. In early December 1961, word gets around among railway employees that a still-open rail connection to Berlin is soon to be blocked off. Harry Deterling resolves to escape immediately to West Berlin on this line by steam train. On 5 December 1961, he tells his relatives and friends the departure time: "The last train to freedom departs today at 7.33 p.m."

At around 8.50 p.m., the train driven by Harry Deterling passes the East German terminus, Albrechtshof, crosses the border and stops on West German territory. As a safety precaution, train driver Deterling and his stoker Hartmut Lichy have climbed into the coal tender while crossing the border; the passengers who know about the escape have thrown themselves onto the floor – but not a shot is fired.

Twenty-five passengers remain in the West; seven return to East Berlin of their own accord. The train is pulled back to the East by a GDR locomotive.

The railway line is closed off the very next day. Tracks are torn up and barriers put in place: the border is made impassable. No train ever succeeds in breaking through the barriers again.

Resignation

Up to the end of 1961, thousands of people are arrested for critical remarks and protests against the building of the Wall. The GDR prisons are so full that even Stasi minister Erich Mielke complains in mid-December 1961, "It is no longer possible to maintain the present high number of arrests." But open protest becomes more rare and silence the rule. Resignation spreads.

"The overall opinion was that the Wall was not right. It would only deepen the rift in Germany further. And I said, if that happens Germany will never be unified again. Those few words cost me 6 months in prison. And I was treated like a dangerous criminal."

Helmut Laetsch, joiner in the state-owned company Holzindustrie Hennigsdorf in 1961.

Evacuated and bricked up – houses on Bernauer Strasse.

4
Escapes / Escape Helpers / Resistance

Escapes / Escape Helpers / Resistance

Between the construction of the Wall and its fall, at least 5,075 GDR citizens succeed in escaping through the border barriers around Berlin, often risking their lives. Many escapees are injured, some of them critically. In Berlin alone, at least 136 people are shot by border soldiers or have fatal accidents. While the barriers and control systems are still provisional, individuals often manage to find ways through the barbed wire. But as the border barriers are extended, it becomes harder – and more dangerous – to escape. In West Berlin, numerous groups form to help escapees. Often they are made up of former escapees who want to bring their relatives, friends and acquaintances over to the West. At first, most of these escape helpers are connected with West Berlin universities. To help fellow students who have been cut off from universities in the West, they look for openings in the border barriers and ways through the underground sewers, detect gaps in the control system at the border crossing points, forge passports, build hiding places in vehicles and dig tunnels under the sector border. The continuous improvement of the barriers and the control system at the border crossings means they have to be constantly on the lookout for new and ever more sophisticated escape routes. And the more sophisticated these are, the more they cost. Even as early as 1962/1963, would-be escapees are often charged between three and five thousand DM.

Precisely because the political reaction at the highest level to the building of the Wall is so helpless and impotent, these actions to help people escape meet with enthusiastic support among the general populace. At first, politicians, and even secret services and police, support them. But as the policy of détente kicks in, there is a change: politicians begin to distance themselves and see such assistance to escape as a disruptive element in negotiations between East and West.

< Previous page: A young woman escapes from Pankow to Reinickendorf via allotments, 25 September 1961.

Hundreds of people escape through the underground sewerage system – until gratings are fitted and the sewers are put under guard, making it necessary to discover new routes.

The GDR border officers are fooled for some time by forged passports and driving licenses from West Berliners, and by fake diplomatic passports. But then the tricks start to be exposed – often revealed by Stasi informers in the West.

Successful escapes from the GDR and East Berlin
through the border barrier system 1961–1989

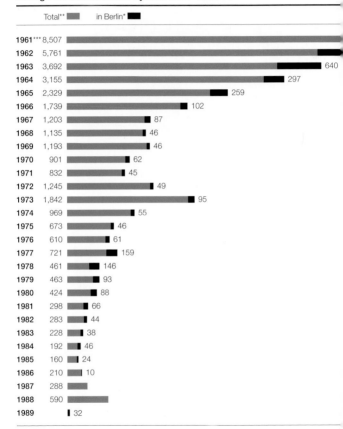

	Total** ▨	in Berlin* ▪
1961***	8,507	
1962	5,761	
1963	3,692	640
1964	3,155	297
1965	2,329	259
1966	1,739	102
1967	1,203	87
1968	1,135	46
1969	1,193	46
1970	901	62
1971	832	45
1972	1,245	49
1973	1,842	95
1974	969	55
1975	673	46
1976	610	61
1977	721	159
1978	461	146
1979	463	93
1980	424	88
1981	298	66
1982	283	44
1983	228	38
1984	192	46
1985	160	24
1986	210	10
1987	288	
1988	590	
1989		32

* Including GDR army deserters; ** no details for 1989
  no details for 1987 and 1988 *** August – December 1961
  annual figures to 13 August each year

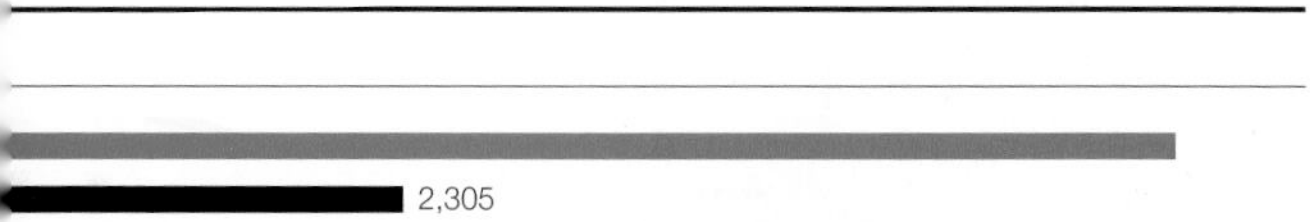

2,305

Successful escapes in Berlin:
at least 5,075

Failed escapes:
unknown

9 December 1961: The death of Dieter Wohlfahrt, a young escape helper

The 20-year-old Austrian Dieter Wohlfahrt is a student at the Technical University in Berlin. After 13 August 1961, he helps many people to escape through the sewerage system, until this underground route is blocked off by gratings.

On 9 December 1961, he and his friends cut through two barbed-wire fences at the border to Staaken to help the mother of an acquaintance to escape. However, the attempt has been betrayed; border police are waiting for the escape helpers and open fire. A bullet hits Dieter Wohlfahrt in the chest. The border policemen leave the critically injured man lying in the border strip for almost an hour without giving assistance. West Berlin policemen and the British military police do not dare to enter the death strip and have to watch on while Dieter Wohlfahrt bleeds to death. GDR sources claim that Dieter Wohlfahrt was armed and shot at border police – something his friends deny.

The "Spiegel" magazine wrote at the time that "Dieter Wohlfahrt was a victim of the bitter realisation that, now all other escape holes have been sealed off, the only remaining way is to break through walls or barbed wire by force. He paid the price that everyone who wants to use this method in future has to bargain with: anyone hit by a burst of submachine-gun fire in the barbed-wire mesh cannot be helped from the West. They will bleed to death, like Dieter Wohlfahrt, in the Dead Zone between East and West."

Tunnel escapes

Digging a tunnel is one of the most time-consuming and arduous ways to escape. Around 40 escape tunnels are known of so far. The first one is built in September 1961; the last futile attempt is made at the end of 1981. Most tunnels are dug by western escape helpers who want to bring over their relatives and friends, but East Germans also dig their own way to the West. Several hundreds of people succeed in escaping underground – but almost as many would-be escapees and escape helpers are arrested and given long prison terms because the attempt was betrayed or discovered.

Escapes by tunnel also cost human lives: two western escape helpers – Heinz Jercha and Siegfried Noffke – are fatally injured by GDR border guards during such escape attempts; two border soldiers also die: Reinhold Huhn is killed by a West Berlin escape helper; Egon Schultz is accidentally shot dead by a fellow soldier.

Several hundreds of East Berliners succeed in escaping by tunnels.

They dig from 6 a.m. to 8 p.m. for 16 days and remove 3,000 buckets of soil from three metres underground: five of the 12 elderly escapees strolling along West Berlin's Kurfürstendamm, 18 May 1962.

5 May 1962: The "Senior Citizens' Tunnel"

"I don't even want to be buried over there," says the 81-year-old leader of a 12-strong group after successfully escaping by tunnel to West Berlin. For 16 days, the group – most of them elderly people – had dug out the 32-metre-long and 1.75-metre-high tunnel, which begins in a small chicken coop on Oranienburger Chaussee in Glienicke and leads to Frohnau in West Berlin. When asked why the tunnel was unusually high, one of the participants explains, "We wanted to walk to freedom with our wives, comfortably and unbowed."

"We wanted to walk to freedom with our wives, comfortably and unbowed."

13 September 1962: Aborted – betrayed – discovered

Most tunnel projects are aborted, betrayed or discovered: on 13 September 1962, GDR border troops uncover a tunnel dug from Heidelberger Strasse in the West Berlin district of Neukölln.

See also: www.chronik-der-mauer.de > English > 1962

Tunnel 29 – a logistical masterpiece. Co-organiser Hasso Herschel helps his sister to escape to the west through the tunnel, along with 28 others.

14 September 1962: Tunnel 29

On 14 and 15 September 1962, a total of 29 GDR citizens flee through a 120-metre-long tunnel built by around 30 helpers from Bernauer Strasse 78/79 (West Berlin) to Schönholzer Strasse 7 (East Berlin).To raise the money for the tunnel, the Italian students Domenico Sesta and Luigi Spina sell the film rights for the tunnel excavation and the arrival of the escapees in the West to the American television station NBC. Helping people to escape as a profitable business? Some of the tunnel-diggers want nothing to do with this idea.

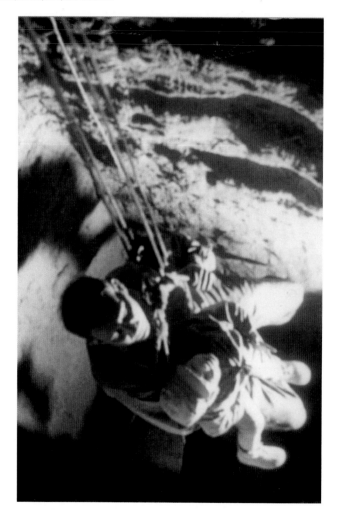

Left and above: Transport to the surface from 12 metres below ground: 57 people escape through this 145-metre-long tunnel on 3 and 4 October 1964.

3 / 4 October 1964: Tunnel 57

On 3 and 4 October 1964, 57 escapees succeed in fleeing through a 145-meter-long tunnel. But on the second day, the tunnel has already been betrayed. When the GDR border guard Egon Schultz is shot dead on 5 October 1964 during a further escape attempt, the escape helpers lose public sympathy – unjustly, as we now know. The GDR exploited this "murder" in its propaganda – and did not reveal that it was not an escape helper, but another border soldier who had fired the fatal shots at Egon Schultz.

Bomb attacks on the Wall

In the first hour of 26 May 1962, explosions at the corner of Bernauer Strasse and Schwedter Strasse tear a large hole in the Wall. A small explosive had been set off shortly before to divert the border police and avoid injury to people. As expected, all available GDR forces hurried to this site, around 300 metres away. Reports from the West Berlin police state that "No offenders could be caught." At the start of 1992, the West Berlin police officer Achim Lazai reveals that two policemen blew up the Wall – in cooperation with escape helpers and with the knowledge of Senate authorities, the head of police and the French military security service. The bomb attack in Bernauer Strasse has many imitators: up to June 1963 alone, 25 attempts to detonate explosives at the Wall are registered in the West. The success rate declines, and soon there is a death: the 22-year-old law student Hans-Jürgen Bischoff dies on 10 May 1963 when he sets off an explosion by accident while working with explosives in his apartment in the West Berlin district of Wilmersdorf.

Official West Berlin authorities withdraw their last support for bomb attacks during talks with the GDR about the possibility of visits in 1963.

Hans-Joachim Lazai, police sergeant in 1962, speaking about his bomb attack of 26 May 1962 "The more massive the Wall became and the more inhumane the situation there was, the stronger became my urge to carry out a conspicuous demonstration. I had the idea of blowing up the Wall and giving the entire world a visible signal. I intended this signal not just to cause a sensation in the West, but also to give the people in the East a sign of hope – you have not been forgotten!"

16 December 1962, 9.15 p.m.: Bomb attack on the Wall in the Kreuzberg district of Berlin, corner of Zimmerstrasse and Jerusalemer Strasse: The East guards the site with a sub-machine gun, the West with a camera.

Escapes through the border barriers

Peter Fechter: Helplessly bleeding to death, 17 August 1962.

Helmut K., Peter Fechter's co-escapee, who reaches West Berlin unharmed, 1962 "Peter Fechter should have been at the Wall before me. I had the feeling when the shots were fired that he was in a state of shock. I called out loudly to him: 'Come on, come on, hurry up!', but he didn't move."

An East German border guard carries the dying Peter Fechter away.

17 August 1962: The agonising death of Peter Fechter

The 18-year-old construction worker Peter Fechter is shot near the Wall while trying to escape and bleeds to death in the border security zone, because no one from the Eastern or the Western side helps him. During the night and the days that follow, outraged West Berliners hold demonstrations and riots against the Wall and the inaction of the American protectors. The next day, the US commandant in West Berlin, Major General Albert E. Watson, calls the event "an act of barbaric inhumanity". From 21 August 1962 on, an Allied ambulance is stationed at Checkpoint Charlie.

See also: www.chronik-der-mauer.de/victims/peter-fechter

" 'Don't shoot!' But he shot anyway." – The stolen armoured car, 17 April 1963.

17 April 1963: Escape in a stolen armoured car

Nineteen-year-old Wolfgang Engels is a trained panel beater and a civilian employee of the National People's Army. On 17 April 1963 he tries to break his way through the Berlin border between Treptow and Neukölln in a stolen Soviet armoured personnel carrier, but becomes trapped in the Wall. Getting out of the car, he at first gets caught in the barbed wire; a border guard opens fire on him. Wolfgang Engels is hit by several bullets. Under the covering fire of a West Berlin policeman, he finally uses his last ounce of strength to climb over the Wall from the bonnet of the car. He is rescued on the West Berlin side with severe injuries.

Wolfgang Engels, 2001 "The armoured car got stuck in the hole in the Wall. I got out and landed right in the barbed wire that I had dragged through with the car. And at that moment a border guard came along. I called out: 'Don't shoot!' But he shot anyway – from a distance of about five metres. The bullet went in through my back and came out the front."

The bus escape fails just before the final barrier – only a metre away from freedom.

12 May 1963: Bus escape fails amid hail of bullets

At midday on 12 May 1963, eight East Berliners aged between 20 and 28 try to break through the cement barriers at the Invalidenstrasse border crossing in a stolen public bus. Border soldiers open fire at the escapees. One hundred and thirty eight shots shatter the Sunday peace. Damaged and unable to manoeuvre, the bus skids into the anti-tank wall – there is only one metre between it and the West.

The driver of the bus, Gerd Keil, and the passengers Gerhard Becker and Manfred Massenthe are seriously injured. When they have recovered, the GDR judiciary takes revenge: they are given prison sentences of ten and nine years respectively. That one metre also costs the other would-be escapees dear. They are sentenced to prison terms of between three and seven and a half years.

January 1965: Escape in a cable drum

In January 1965, six people escape hidden in wooden cable drums belonging the Berlin Electricity Works, transported from West Berlin to West Germany by haulage contractors along the transit route.

Finding the way across the death strip looking through a steel sheet with small peepholes – the tree is on West Berlin territory.

11 September 1966: Escape by bulldozer

Two married couples with a three-year-old child break through the border in Staaken using a 12-ton bulldozer – originally used to clear weeds from the death strip.

The cabin of the bulldozer and the fuel injection pump are protected by steel sheets. The vehicle destroys an alarm fence and flattens several mesh fences. Border troops fire 60 shots at the bulldozer – two of the adults are slightly grazed by bullets. Finally, the vehicle is stopped by a tree – to the joy of the escapees, it is on West Berlin territory.

7 July 1969: The Trojan Cow

A "Trojan Cow" has already brought escapees to the West twice. But on a third attempt, the trick is discovered. In the evening of 7 July 1969, two escape helpers transport the bull, built as a display item, by van on the transit motorway to West Berlin. 18-year-old Angelika B. from Karl-Marx-Stadt (now Chemnitz) joins them on the way; she wants to live with her West Berlin fiancé in the West. She hides in the hollow body of the animal, which is housed in a wooden crate. Her fiancé has paid 5,000 DM for the escape; if it is successful, he will have to pay another 5,000.

But at the Drewitz border crossing, the hiding place is discovered and the trio is arrested and taken to the Stasi remand jail in Lindenstrasse in Potsdam. On 15 October 1969, the Potsdam District Court sentences the escape helpers to more than three years' imprisonment "for subversive people trafficking". Angelika B. is given a prison sentence of two years and ten months for attempted "illegal border crossing". After four months she is ransomed by West Germany.

Angelika B., 2004 "The controllers picked out the van from the back of the queue. This proves that the escape had been betrayed and they were waiting for us. They stood there with spotlights and photographed us."

* Don't get cheeky, Mr Brandt, we're good shots.

Nicht frech werden, Herr Brandt, wir sind gute Schützen.

* The peoples' call for détente will prevail.

Der Ruf der Völker nach Entspannung wird sich durchsetzen!

5
Confrontation and Détente

Confrontation and Détente

The Wall divides up the superpowers' spheres of influence in Europe. No further escalation – such as blocking off the connecting routes to Berlin – occurs. The nuclear balance that arises between the Soviet Union and the USA means both sides are constrained in their actions and willingness to take risks.

With the Wall built and the flow of refugees checked, the Soviet Union feels that the trouble spot of Berlin has been brought under control and the existence of the GDR has been secured. Much to Ulbricht's disappointment, Khrushchev abandons his most ambitious objectives. The main arena of the Cold War shifts to Asia, Africa and Latin America in the 1960s. Owing to ideological and military tensions with the People's Republic of China, the Soviet Union tries to bring calm to the European front and to press for recognition of the status quo from the West. In the GDR, the majority of the population is compelled to face up to its imprisonment behind the Wall and life under a dictatorship. Anyone who has been hoping that there will now come a phase of "socialist construction" and "normalisation" and that the Wall will disappear as soon as the GDR is stabilised is disappointed. The SED leadership is not even thinking about constructing a political system that would make the Wall redundant. The Wall is – and, until 1989, remains – a condition of existence for the GDR.

In West Germany and in West Berlin, the construction of the Wall becomes the "hour of great disillusionment", destroying all hopes that the SED regime might soon fall. The border-pass negotiations between the West Berlin Senate and the GDR government and the ransoming of political prisoners from 1963 on mark the beginning of a policy of "humane alleviation" and "small steps". GDR representatives are accepted as negotiating partners and there is no more reliance on a destabilisation of the GDR. A new leitmotif of ostpolitik under West German Chancellor Willy Brandt is "to recognise

< Previous page: The Wall in Berlin-Mitte, Wilhelmstrasse, late 1961.

the division in order to ease its consequences for the people." West Germany's claim to be the sole representative of all Germany is gradually dropped. In 1972, West Germany recognises the GDR as an independent state in the German-German Basic Treaty, and accepts the inviolability of its national border. The two German states continue to hold different views on various fundamental political issues: in 1967, East Berlin announces its own GDR citizenship and in 1974 it removes all references to a common German nation from the GDR constitution. Bonn, on the other hand, adheres to the idea of a common citizenship and remains committed to the goal of reunification. But German unity recedes into the distant future.

"All free men, wherever they may live, are citizens of Berlin, and, therefore, as a free man, I take pride in the words: Ich bin ein Berliner."

John F. Kennedy in West Berlin, 26 June 1963.

Ish bin ein Bearleener

President John F. Kennedy's speech card, 26 June 1963.

John F. Kennedy (center) with Konrad Adenauer (right) and Willy Brandt (2nd from right) on the west side of Friedrichstrasse crossing point ("Checkpoint Charlie"), 26 June 1963.

Nikita Khrushchev (center) with Walter Ulbricht (covered) on the east side of the Friedrichstrasse crossing point ("Checkpoint Charlie"), 17 January 1963.

Khrushchev and Kennedy in Berlin

In 1963, the leaders of the two superpowers travel to Berlin: Khrushchev to East Berlin, Kennedy to West Berlin. Both statesmen visit the Wall – but they do not cross the border. In October 1962 they were on the brink of nuclear war when the Soviet Union stationed medium-range missiles in Cuba – only 90 miles away from the coast of Florida. By threatening to use atomic weapons, Kennedy managed to persuade Khrushchev to withdraw the missiles. At the same time, however, he also had to promise to withdraw US missiles from Turkey – and not to attack communist Cuba again. The trial of strength ended inconclusively. Since then, a "hotline" has connected Moscow and Washington; it is meant to help avoid misunderstandings and misinterpretations by the other side. Now, in Berlin, Khrushchev and Kennedy call on their German allies to recognise the realities of the situation to keep things calm.

At an SED conference in East Berlin on 16 January 1963, Khrushchev, reacting to the constant requests by Ulbricht for Soviet help, demands an increase in productivity in the GDR: "Neither God nor the devil will give you bread or butter if you do not manage it with your own hands. […] We must not expect alms from some rich uncle." His message is that the GDR should help itself and stabilise itself economically.

Kennedy, on the other hand, demands in West Berlin that people face up to facts and no longer fall prey to self-deception: "We all know that a police state regime has been imposed on the Eastern sector of this city and country. The peaceful reunification of Berlin and Germany will, therefore, not be either quick or easy. […] But in the meantime, justice requires us to do what we can do in this transition period to improve the lot and maintain the hopes of those on the other side." The wind of change, he says, is blowing across the Iron Curtain. He urges that Western policies should be directed at alleviating the consequences of the division for the people.

Five months later, on 22 November 1963, John F. Kennedy is murdered in Dallas, USA. Nikita Khrushchev is removed from office on 14 October 1964.

State Visits to the Wall, West.

State Visits to the Wall, East.

Cell in the Potsdam Stasi remand prison, Lindenstrasse 54/55. The East German secret service operates a total of 17 remand prisons for political prisoners across the GDR.

< Previous Page: State visits to the Wall. In the 1960s, the Wall becomes a site of political pilgrimages: the West shows its state guests the "communist wall of shame" that has locked in the people of the GDR. The East shows its visitors the "anti-fascist protective wall" that has locked out the imperialists.
West (left page): British Prime Minister Harold Wilson (left) with Willy Brandt (2nd from left) on Potsdamer Platz, 6 March 1965. / Hamani Diori, President of Niger (left) on Potsdamer Platz, 12 March 1965. / The US astronauts Neill Armstrong, Michael Collins and Edwin Aldrin at the Wall, 13 October 1969.
East (right page): The Soviet cosmonaut Gherman Titov at the Brandenburg Gate, 1 September 1961. / Yasser Arafat, head of the Palestinian Liberation Organisation (4th from left), 2 November 1971. / Fidel Castro, head of the Cuban Communist Party and government, with the SED politburo member Werner Lamberz (2nd from left), 14 June 1972.

Ransoming of prisoners

At the start of the 1960s, around 12,000 political prisoners in GDR prisons are known to the West German government by name. Often given draconian sentences by the SED judiciary, they have little hope of being released any time in the near future. Since the 1950s, various West German organisations have been trying to gain their release – in vain.

In 1963, after laborious negotiations, the GDR first agrees to sell eight prisoners to West Germany for 205,000 DM in cash. With this deal, both German states successfully test whether the other side is willing and capable of keeping this human trafficking confidential. After this, the GDR indicates that it is prepared to sell between 500 and 1,500 political prisoners to the Federal Republic every year. The negotiator for the East is the lawyer Dr. Wolfgang Vogel and for the West the Federal Ministry for All-German (later: Inner-German) Affairs. The ransomed prisoners are usually transported from East Germany to West Germany by bus via the Herleshausen border crossing. They are constrained to complete silence so as not to endanger future transactions.

95,847 DM ransom per prisoner

The price for each prisoner is negotiated on an individual basis – depending on their professional training and the severity of the sentence. In the mid-1960s, an average price of 40,000 DM per prisoner replaces the individual prices; by the end of the 1980s, this is raised to 95,847 DM. The payment is no longer made in cash, but in the form of goods delivered via the Social Service Agency of the German Protestant Church. For the GDR, the sale of prisoners is an important and reliable source of foreign currency, as its politically founded criminal law ensures that new prisoners are in constant supply.

Border-pass agreement

A border-pass agreement between the West Berlin Senate and the East Berlin authorities allows West Berliners to visit their relatives over Christmas and New Year 1963/64 for the first time since the construction of the Wall.

730,000 people put up with long processing periods and make applications: 1.2 million visits to East Berlin are registered between 19 December and 5 January.

Border-pass agreements for periods of between two and three weeks follow in 1964, 1965 and 1966. On 29 July 1966, negotiations on a further agreement break down because the GDR refuses to accept the previous preamble – both sides come to the conclusion that they cannot reach agreement on the terms for locations, authorities and offices – and demands recognition under international law. For six long years – until 1972 – West Berliners are not allowed to visit their East Berlin relatives, apart from a few exceptions.

See also: www.chronik-der-mauer.de > Chronik > 1963 > Rias Reportage (German audio)

West Berliners are allowed to visit their relatives over Christmas and New Year 1963/64 for the first time since the construction of the Wall. 1.2 million visits are made in only 18 days.

An emotional reunion, Christmas 1963.

German-German summit in Erfurt

In the wake of the American-Soviet policy of détente, the first German-German summit takes place on 19 March 1970. The Chairman of the GDR Council of Ministers, Willi Stoph, demands the establishment of relations under international law between the GDR and the FRG; West German Chancellor Willy Brandt, on the other hand, insists on special German-German relations. The differences are irreconcilable.

In front of the Erfurter Hof Hotel, where the meeting takes place, several thousand people break through the barriers put up by the Stasi and chant "Willy, Willy". Then the crowd calls: "Willy Brandt to the window!" leaving no doubt as to which Willy is the object of their support. "I did not obey at first," Willy Brandt later wrote, "but then I did so, gesturing with my hands to call for restraint. I was moved and realised that they were one people with me. How strong the feeling of belonging must have been that found an outlet like this."

The "Erfurt incident" strengthens the mistrust of the Soviet leadership with regard to Walter Ulbricht's policies on Germany. Ever since the social-liberal coalition was formed in West Germany, the top brass of the CPSU has felt a growing suspicion that the SED Secretary-General could be oriented towards a too close connection with the West German Social Democrats – disregarding the Soviet Union. "What does Walter want with the possibility, a possibility that cannot be proven by any means, of cooperation with the West German Social Democrats; what does he understand by the demand to help Brandt's government? Well, you don't know and I don't know either!" complains CPSU General Secretary Brezhnev in a one-to-one conversation with Erich Honecker. And then he impresses on Ulbricht's designated successor: "Erich, let me tell you quite frankly, never forget this: the GDR cannot exist without us, without the Soviet Union, its power and strength. Without us there is no GDR. […] There must not be any process of rapprochement between the FRG and the GDR."

At the Eighth SED Party Congress in April 1971, Ulbricht is relieved of his duties – his successor is Erich Honecker. Honecker immediately assures Brezhnev "that we remain firmly in a position of complete class dissociation from the imperialist FRG, as we agreed." He says the SED will continue with the line of economic independence from West Germany so as not to end up being politically dependent.

Finally, three agreements pave the way for a treaty policy between the two German states:

On 12 August 1970, in Moscow, the Federal Republic of Germany and the Soviet Union sign a treaty on the renunciation of force and the normalisation of relations. In the treaty, both states give up territorial claims and agree "[to consider] the borders of all states in Europe to be inviolable in the future […] including the Oder-Neisse line […] and the border between the Federal Republic of Germany and the German Democratic Republic." West German Foreign Minister Walter Scheel afterwards explains in the so-called "Letter on German Unity", which becomes a part of the treaty, that the "treaty does not contradict the political aim of the Federal Republic of Germany to work towards a state of peace in Europe in which the German people will be able to regain their unity in free self-determination."

In the Treaty of Warsaw with Poland on 7 December 1970, West Germany recognises the Oder-Neisse line as the western border of Poland.

On 3 September 1971, the USA and the USSR, Great Britain and France finally sign the Four-Power Agreement on Berlin. On the basis of the continuing four-power status for all of Berlin, the rights and responsibilities of the three powers for the West sectors of Berlin and the connections between the West sectors of Berlin and the Federal Republic are confirmed. The Soviet Union guarantees that civilian traffic between West Berlin and West Germany will be able to pass easily and quickly without hindrance in future. The agreement of concrete regulations is left up to the relevant German authorities.

* Those who attack us will be destroyed.

WER UNS
ANGREIFT
WIRD
VERNICHTET

6
Perfecting
the Border Barrier System

Perfecting the Border Barrier System

Year by year, the barrier system through the middle of Berlin is made more sophisticated. From 1962, it is guarded according to military principles: by the border troops of the GDR. Along with the barriers and guards, the third element in the military protection of the border is shooting at escapees.

In the first year of the Wall's existence, the Berlin border brigades are under the command of the GDR Interior Ministry. Their lack of discipline is a source of irritation to the SED leadership. Every day, several escapes succeed; 77 border policemen alone cross to the West in 1962. The National Defence Council notes that not all border guards have recognised that "border violators [should be] captured as enemies at all costs, and if necessary exterminated." Calls from the West like "Shoot to miss – don't become a murderer" are said to have had their effect.

For this reason, in August 1962 the Berlin border units are put under the command of the Ministry for National Defence. From now on, the border guards are drilled to obey orders and given military training. The cooperation between the border troops and the Stasi and People's Police is improved so that escape attempts can be found out and prevented at the planning stage. The Stasi has full-time staff infiltrate the border troops and recruits "unofficial employees" to prevent desertions. In the area near the border, collaborators ("voluntary helpers") are found who help watch over the people living there.

From the mid-1960s, the extension of the border barriers is no longer carried out in makeshift fashion, but according to standardised military plans. Elements of the system such as concrete slabs and watchtowers are produced on an assembly line. By the end of the 1960s, start of the 1970s, a nearly impregnable border security system has been created.

< Previous page: Berlin-Mitte, Wilhelmstrasse/Niederkirchnerstrasse, August 1962.

Installing electric alarm fences, 1964.

Replacing barbed wire with wire mesh fencing, 1965.

Installing spiked gratings ("Stalin's lawn") in the death strip between Treptow and Neukölln (Bouchéstrasse).

"Border violators [should be] captured as enemies at all costs, and if necessary exterminated."

National Defence Council, East Germany, September 1962.

Raised hunting hide for spotting escapees in the death strip between Kreuzberg and Friedrichshain, October 1963.

Four generations of the Wall

The first and second generations of the Wall (made from breeze-blocks or concrete slabs for road construction) are followed, in the second half of the 1960s, by the Wall of the third generation built of prefabricated slabs.

From the mid-1970s, the fourth-generation Wall is built. It consists of industrially produced, vertically erected concrete segments, which were previously used in agriculture: as walls for storing liquid manure.

Wall made from breeze-blocks (1st generation) between Treptow and Neukölln (Elsenstrasse), April 1963. < East / West >

Construction of the 3rd generation of the Wall, built of prefabricated slabs, between Kreuzberg and Friedrichshain, 1966. < West / East >

2nd and 3rd generation of the Wall, July 1966.

4th generation of the Wall, combined with anti-tank obstacles, in the mid 1980s.

4th generation of the Wall between Berlin-Mitte and Kreuzberg (Sebastianstrasse),
in the mid 1980s. < West / East >

The barrier system

From east to west, the death strip, between 15 and more than 150 metres in width, begins with a two-to-three-metre-high so-called "hinterland" barrier, the wall or fence nearest to East Berlin territory. An electrified signal fence, a good two metres high, follows at a short distance. This "contact fence" is equipped with several rows of wires that are live and send out acoustic and/or optical signals. The more technically developed versions of this fence, like the "Grenzsignal- und Sperrzaun II", are driven fifty centimetres deep into the soil to make it more difficult to crawl underneath. In the modern fence systems, the alarm triggered is a silent one: while escapees think they are still safe, they have already been located by the command centre for that segment of the border.

Parallel to the signal fence, there are runs for chained dogs in spots that are hard to watch over.

Then comes the segment with the watchtowers and bunkers for the border soldiers and a patrol route for the motorised patrols. The cable duct for the border communication system mostly runs alongside the patrol route. A line of lights brightly illuminates the death strip so that the guards have good visibility and good shooting conditions at night as well.

The last obstacle before the Wall is the anti-vehicle trench, which slants down away from the GDR side but is vertical on the side of the border and partly reinforced with cement slabs.

The final element in this system of barriers is a concrete wall, 3.5-to-4-metres high and ten centimetres thick, with a pipe on top that is meant to make it more difficult to find handholds when climbing over; its function is some-times taken over by a 2.9-metre-high mesh fence.

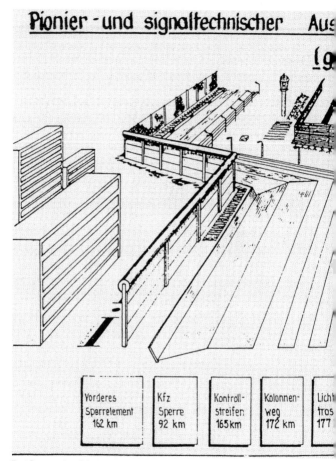

Pionier - und signaltechnischer Aus

[g

Vorderes Sperrelement 162 km	Kfz Sperre 92 km	Kontroll- streifen 165km	Kolonnen- weg 172 km	Licht tros 177

East German plan of the inner-city barrier system, 1970s: "Technical and signalling enhancements to the state border to Berlin-West": front border wall, anti-vehicle trench, security strip, patrol route, line of lights,

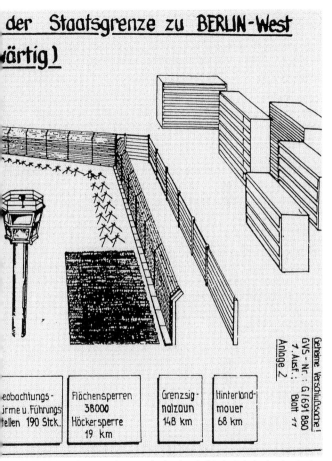

der Staatsgrenze zu BERLIN-West

ärtig)

| eobachtungs-
ürme u.Führungs
tellen 190 Stck. | Flächensperren
38000
Höckersperre
19 km | Grenzsig-
nalzaun
148 km | Hinterland-
mouer
68 km |

Geheime Verschlußsache!
GVS - Nr.: G I 691 880
7. Ausf.:
Blatt 11
Anlage 2

watchtowers and command posts, spiked gratings/anti-tank obstacles, border signal
fence, inner blocking wall".

115

Costs of the Wall

The barrier systems put up in Berlin until 1970 alone cost around 100 million GDR-marks – which does not include the personnel costs for their surveillance.

To this day, it is not known how many billions the Wall swallowed up until 1989. Internal records on the total annual expenditure for GDR border troops show it climbing from 600 million marks in 1970 to almost one billion marks in 1983. In the spring of 1989, economists for the border troops draw up a grotesque calculation: they divide the costs for the border by the number of arrests and discover that each arrest costs 2.1 million marks. They estimate the value of an average working person at 700,000 marks. The cost of an arrest is thus three times as high as the value of the prisoner, they reason. They conclude that securing the border had to be made cheaper.

Guarding the border in Berlin is part of a large (secret) police and military complex, the immense cost of which helps drive the GDR into bankruptcy in the 1980s. No other Eastern Bloc country uses a higher proportion of its national income for military expenditure than the GDR; it amounts to 957 marks per capita in the 1980s, three times as high as in the Soviet Union (322 marks).

With a population of just under 17 million, there are almost a million men in the armed forces in the GDR, including the Soviet troops.

Citizens of the GDR:
16,9 million

Armed forces in the GDR:
0.933 million

Combat Groups military parade on the fifth anniversary of the Wall's construction, East Berlin, 13 August 1966.

The border troops as part of the (secret) police and military dictatorship

Armed Bodies	Number of Personnel
National People's Army	173,000
Border troops	50,000
Ministry for State Security	91,000
German People's Police	60,000
Combat Groups	209,000
Subtotal	**583,000**
Soviet Armed Forces in the GDR	350,000
Total	**933,000**

November 1989

The border troops

From 1971, the border units responsible for securing the 156.4-kilometre-long Berlin Wall are under the command of the Centre Border Command, headquartered in the Karlshorst district of Berlin. Together with the Border Commands South and North, responsible respectively for the inner-German border, it is under the command of the 50,000-strong Border Troop Command.

In 1989, the Centre Border Command is made up of around 11,000 soldiers: some 2,400 regular officers – mostly members of the SED – 1,700 non-commissioned officers on temporary contracts and 7,200 conscripts. Three of its seven border regiments are stationed in Berlin, four in the Potsdam district. Two training regiments stationed on the edge of Berlin in Oranienburg and Wilhelmshagen – train the border soldiers during basic military service. All nine regiments are made up of 1,000 to 1,400 soldiers each.

Distance between the sentries (in the middle of the city): 320 metres during the day, 260 metres at night.

Guarding the border is carried out in six to ten-hour shifts, with the five companies of a border regiment on duty one after the other. Around 100 men guard the border segments, between 12.7 km (Border Regiment 35) and 29.8 km (Border Regiment 38) long. The distance between the sentries in the middle of the city is 320 metres on average during the day, and 260 metres at night; where border control is tighter, the distance between the sentries is reduced to 260 metres during the day and 150 metres at night. In the Potsdam area, the sentries stand further apart: between 560 and

950 metres during the day, and 400 to 650 at night and when tighter controls are in place.

The Central Border Command and its regiments are equipped with 2,295 vehicles, 10,726 submachine guns, 600 light and heavy machine guns, 2,753 pistols, 29 border-security boats and 992 tracker and guard dogs.

But they are also provided with heavy weapons and technology: 567 armoured halftracks, 48 mortars, 48 anti-tank guns, 114 flamethrowers, 682 anti-tank rifles, 156 armoured cars and heavy field engineering equipment.

For, in addition to securing the border, the Central Border Command has another responsibility: to take over West Berlin if war breaks out, together with Soviet armed forces and units of the National People's Army ("Berliner Gruppierung") – within 24 hours, according to plans. For this reason, staff officers regularly practise the capture of West Berlin in war games – and the units of the border regiments are trained for war operations.

Border soldiers starting work on the death strip – every two soldiers guard each other, 1980s.

The "order to shoot" – license to kill

Along with nearly insurmountable barriers and a dense deployment of border guards, shooting to kill escapees is the third and decisive element of the GDR border regime. The only adequate way for the SED regime to prevent escapes in the long term is to threaten the death penalty – and to carry it out if necessary. In the trials that began in 1990s in connection with the fatal shootings of escapees, the members of the former political and military leadership of the GDR vehemently denied that there had even been an "order to shoot". In a strict legal sense, they were right, as the laws, regulations and orders regarding the use of firearms only provided permission, and did not impose an obligation, to deliver fatal shots.

But laws in the GDR are subject to political opportunism. Politically motivated penal laws that define escape attempts under certain circumstances as an offence, ideological indoctrination that teaches the young soldiers to feel unconditional hate for the "border violators", and commendations and bonuses for people who fired fatal shots make "permission" almost tanta-mount to an obligation.

Kalashnikov AK-47 submachine gun, 30-round detachable box magazine, effective semi-automatic and fully automatic range of 300–400 metres.

"Border violators are to be arrested or exterminated" – it is with this order that the GDR border soldiers are sent to their posts in the death strip every day until well into the 1980s. As Erich Honecker states in 1974, "firearms are to be ruthlessly used in the event of attempts to break through the border, and the comrades who have successfully used their firearms are to be commended."

But when it doesn't suit the SED politically for shooting to take place at the border – for example, in the case of international events or state visits where the GDR is in the limelight – the order to shoot is temporarily suspended.

"Anyone who does not respect our border will feel the bullet."

GDR Defence Minister Heinz Hoffmann, August 1966.

Protests against the killing of escapees meet with more response from SED leaders, the more the GDR courts international recognition and finally, in the 1980s, becomes economically dependent on the West. On 3 April 1989, Honecker gives the order that "firearms [are] no longer to be used to prevent border breakthroughs." The international isolation threatening the GDR after the fatal shooting of Chris Gueffroy begins to take effect. "Better to let someone get away than to use firearms in the current political situation," SED General Secretary Erich Honecker tells his military officers. The order to shoot, a condition for the existence of the SED state, is thus revoked. Not much later, the GDR disappears.

7
Deaths
at the Berlin Wall

Deaths at the Berlin Wall

Between 1961 and 1989, at least 138 people are killed at the Berlin Wall or die from causes related to the GDR border regime. An unknown number of people die out of worry and desperation over the effects of the Wall on their own lives.

At least this many people lose their lives at the Berlin Wall:
- 100 GDR citizens who are shot, have a fatal accident or kill themselves while trying to escape through, over or under the border installations,
- 30 people from the East and West who are not intending to escape but are shot or have fatal accidents,
- 8 GDR border soldiers killed on duty.

In addition, numerous, mostly elderly, travellers die during or after inspections at the border crossings in Berlin, mostly from heart attacks.

Killings and murders at the Berlin Wall – as well as on the inner German border, at the Baltic Sea and and on the borders to third countries – are the most extreme cases of violence connected with the protection of the GDR's border. The SED leadership sanctions the killings. But it also knows that shootings and deaths on the border – especially in periods of détente – are not good for the GDR's international reputation. For this reason, it tries, together with the border troops and the state security police, to keep deaths secret and cover up whenever possible. The Stasi even has bodies disappear without trace. Many families do not learn about the circumstances of their relatives' deaths until the 1990s – after the GDR archives have been opened and during criminal investigations of the acts of violence.

< Previous Page: From left to right, 1st row: Günter Litfin, Hans Räwel, Hildegard Trabant, Michael Kollender, Eduard Wroblewski, Karl-Heinz-Kube;
2nd row: Giuseppe Savoca, Cetin Mert, Herbert Kiebler, Ulrich Steinhauer, Marienetta Jirkowsky, Rainer Liebeke;
3rd row: Lutz Schmidt, Chris Gueffroy, Winfried Freudenberg.

Escapees who are shot, have a fatal accident or commit suicide at the Berlin Wall between 1961 and 1989; people not intending to escape who are shot or have a fatal accident in the border area

1961

Ida Siekmann	Age 58	*23.08.1902	† 22.08.1961	Fatally injured while trying to escape
Günter Litfin	Age 24	*19.01.1937	† 24.08.1961	Shot while trying to escape
Roland Hoff	Age 27	*19.03.1934	† 29.08.1961	Shot while trying to escape
Rudolf Urban	Age 47	*06.06.1914	† 17.09.1961	Died from injuries incurred while trying to escape
Olga Segler	Age 80	*31.07.1881	† 26.09.1961	Died from injuries incurred while trying to escape
Bernd Lünser	Age 22	*11.03.1939	† 04.10.1961	Fatally injured under fire while trying to escape
Udo Düllick	Age 25	*03.08.1936	† 05.10.1961	Drowned under fire while trying to escape
Werner Probst	Age 26	*18.06.1936	† 14.10.1961	Shot while trying to escape
Lothar Lehmann	Age 19	*28.01.1942	† 26.11.1961	Drowned while trying to escape
Dieter Wohlfahrt	Age 20	*27.05.1941	† 09.12.1961	Shot while helping others to escape
Ingo Krüger	Age 21	*31.01.1940	† 11.12.1961	Drowned while trying to escape
Georg Feldhahn	Age 20	*12.08.1941	† 19.12.1961	Drowned while trying to escape

1962

Dorit Schmiel	Age 20	*25.04.1941	† 19.02.1962	Shot while trying to escape
Heinz Jercha	Age 27	*01.07.1934	† 27.03.1962	Shot while helping others to escape
Philipp Held	Age 19	*02.05.1942	† April 1962	Drowned while trying to escape
Klaus Brueske	Age 23	*14.09.1938	† 18.04.1962	Shot while trying to escape
Peter Böhme	Age 19	*17.08.1942	† 18.04.1962	Shot while trying to escape
Horst Frank	Age 19	*07.05.1942	† 29.04.1962	Shot while trying to escape
Lutz Haberlandt	Age 24	*29.04.1938	† 27.05.1962	Shot while trying to escape
Axel Hannemann	Age 17	*27.04.1945	† 05.06.1962	Shot while trying to escape
Erna Kelm	Age 53	*21.07.1908	† 11.06.1962	Drowned while trying to escape
Wolfgang Glöde	Age 13	*01.02.1949	† 11.06.1962	Accidentally shot while playing in the border area
Siegfried Noffke	Age 22	*09.12.1939	† 28.06.1962	Shot while helping others to escape
Peter Fechter	Age 18	*14.01.1944	† 17.08.1962	Shot while trying to escape

Hans-Dieter Wesa	Age 19	*10.01.1943	†23.08.1962	Shot while trying to escape
Ernst Mundt	Age 41	*02.12.1921	†04.09.1962	Shot while trying to escape
Anton Walzer	Age 60	*27.04.1902	†08.10.1962	Shot while trying to escape
Horst Plischke	Age 23	*12.07.1939	†19.11.1962	Drowned while trying to escape
Ottfried Reck	Age 17	*14.12.1944	†27.11.1962	Shot while trying to escape
Günter Wiedenhöft	Age 20	*14.02.1942	†06.12.1962	Drowned while trying to escape

1963

Hans Räwel	Age 21	*11.12.1941	†01.01.1963	Shot while trying to escape
Horst Kutscher	Age 31	*05.07.1931	†15.01.1963	Shot while trying to escape
Peter Kreitlow	Age 20	*15.01.1943	†24.01.1963	Shot while trying to escape
Wolf-Olaf Muszynski	Age 16	*01.02.1947	†Feb.1963	Drowned while trying to escape
Peter Mädler	Age 19	*10.07.1943	†26.04.1963	Shot while trying to escape
Klaus Schröter	Age 23	*21.02.1940	†04.11.1963	Shot at while trying to escape and drowned due to injuries
Dietmar Schulz	Age 24	*21.10.1939	†25.11.1963	Fatally injured while trying to escape
Dieter Berger	Age 24	*27.10.1939	†13.12.1963	Shot while trying to escape
Paul Schultz	Age 18	*02.10.1945	†25.12.1963	Shot while trying to escape

1964

Walter Hayn	Age 25	*31.01.1939	†27.02.1964	Shot while trying to escape
Adolf Philipp	Age 20	*17.08.1943	†05.05.1964	West Berliner Shot in the border area
Walter Heike	Age 29	*20.09.1934	†22.06.1964	Shot while trying to escape
Norbert Wolscht	Age 20	*27.10.1943	†28.07.1964	Drowned while trying to escape
Rainer Gneiser	Age 20	*10.01.1944	†28.07.1964	Drowned while trying to escape
Hildegard Trabant	Age 37	*12.06.1927	†18.08.1964	Shot dead while trying to escape
Wernhard Mispelhorn	Age 18	*10.11.1945	†20.08.1964	Shot at while trying to escape and died of his injuries
Hans-Joachim Wolf	Age 17	*08.08.1947	†26.11.1964	Shot while trying to escape
Joachim Mehr	Age 19	*03.04.1945	†03.12.1964	Shot while trying to escape

1965

| Unidentified fugitive | | | †19.01.1965 | Drowned while trying to escape |
| Christian Buttkus | Age 21 | *21.02.1944 | †04.03.1965 | Shot while trying to escape |

Ulrich Krzemien	Age 24	* 13. 09. 1940	† 25. 03. 1965	Drowned as a West Berliner in border waters
Peter Hauptmann	Age 26	* 20. 03. 1939	† 03. 05. 1965	Shot in the border area with no intent to escape
Hermann Döbler	Age 42	* 28. 10. 1922	† 15. 06. 1965	West Berliner shot in the border area
Klaus Kratzel	Age 25	* 03. 03. 1940	† 08. 08. 1965	Fatally injured while trying to escape
Klaus Garten	Age 24	* 19. 07. 1941	† 18. 08. 1965	Shot while trying to escape
Walter Kittel	Age 22	* 21. 11. 1942	† 18. 10. 1965	Shot while trying to escape
Heinz Cyrus	Age 29	* 05. 06. 1936	† 11. 11. 1965	Fatally injured under fire while trying to escape
Heinz Sokolowski	Age 47	* 17. 12. 1917	† 25. 11. 1965	Shot while trying to escape
Erich Kühn	Age 62	* 27. 02. 1903	† 03. 12. 1965	Shot while trying to escape
Heinz Schöneberger	Age 27	* 07. 06. 1938	† 26. 12. 1965	Shot while helping others to escape

1966

Dieter Brandes	Age 19	* 23. 10. 1946	† 11. 01. 1966	Shot at while trying to escape and died of his injuries
Willi Block	Age 31	* 05. 06. 1934	† 07. 02. 1966	Shot while trying to escape
Jörg Hartmann	Age 10	* 27. 10. 1955	† 14. 03. 1966	Shot while trying to escape
Lothar Schleusener	Age 13	* 14. 01. 1953	† 14. 03. 1966	Shot while trying to escape
Willi Marzahn	Age 21	* 03. 06. 1944	† 19. 03. 1966	Shot while trying to escape or committed suicide
Eberhard Schulz	Age 20	* 11. 03. 1946	† 30. 03. 1966	Shot while trying to escape
Michael Kollender	Age 21	* 19. 02. 1945	† 25. 04. 1966	Shot while trying to escape
Paul Stretz	Age 31	* 28. 02. 1935	† 29. 04. 1966	West Berliner shot in the border area
Eduard Wroblewski	Age 33	* 03. 03. 1933	† 26. 07. 1966	Shot while trying to escape
Heinz Schmidt	Age 46	* 26. 10. 1919	† 29. 08. 1966	West Berliner shot in the border area
Andreas Senk	Age 5/6	* 1960	† 13. 09. 1966	Drowned in border waters
Karl-Heinz Kube	Age 17	* 10. 04. 1949	† 16. 12. 1966	Shot while trying to escape

1967

| Max Sahmland | Age 37 | * 28. 03. 1929 | † 27. 01. 1967 | Shot at while trying to escape and drowned because of his injuries |
| Franciszek Piesik | Age 24 | * 23. 11. 1942 | † 17. 10. 1967 | Drowned while trying to escape |

1968

Elke Weckeiser	Age 22	*31.10.1945	†18.02.1968	Shot while trying to escape
Dieter Weckeiser	Age 25	*15.02.1943	†19.02.1968	Shot while trying to escape
Herbert Mende	Age 29	*09.02.1939	†10.03.1968	Shot while trying to escape
Bernd Lehmann	Age 18	*31.07.1949	†28.05.1968	Drowned while trying to escape
Siegfried Krug	Age 28	*22.07.1939	†06.07.1968	Shot as a West Berliner in the border area
Horst Körner	Age 21	*12.07.1947	†15.11.1968	Shot while trying to escape

1969

Johannes Lange	Age 28	*17.12.1940	†09.04.1969	Shot while trying to escape
Klaus-Jürgen Kluge	Age 21	*25.07.1948	†13.09.1969	Shot while trying to escape
Leo Lis	Age 45	*10.05.1924	†20.09.1969	Shot while trying to escape

1970

Christel Wehage	Age 23	*15.12.1946	†10.03.1970	Committed suicide after a failed escape with a hijacked airplane
Eckhard Wehage	Age 21	*08.07.1948	†10.03.1970	Committed suicide after a failed escape with a hijacked airplane
Heinz Müller	Age 27	*16.05.1943	†19.06.1970	Shot as a West Berliner in the border area
Willi Born	Age 19	*19.07.1950	†07.07.1970	Committed suicide after a failed escape attempt
Friedhelm Ehrlich	Age 20	*11.07.1950	†02.08.1970	Shot with no intent to escape
Gerald Thiem	Age 41	*06.09.1928	†07.08.1970	West Berliner shot in the border area
Hans-Joachim Zock	Age 30	*26.01.1940	†Nov. 1970	Drowned while trying to escape
Helmut Kliem	Age 31	*02.06.1939	†13.11.1970	Shot in the border area with no intent to escape
Christian Peter Friese	Age 22	*05.01.1948	†25.12.1970	Shot while trying to escape

1971

Rolf-Dieter Kabelitz	Age 19	*23.06.1951	†30.01.1971	Shot at during an escape attempt and died of his injuries
Wolfgang Hoffmann	Age 28	*01.09.1942	†15.07.1971	West Berliner fatally injured after being arrested in East Berlin

| Werner Kühl | Age 22 | *10.02.1949 | †24.07.1971 | West Berliner Shot in the border area |
| Dieter Beilig | Age 30 | *05.09.1941 | †02.10.1971 | West Berliner Shot in the border area |

1972

Horst Kullack	Age 23	*20.11.1948	†21.01.1972	Shot at while trying to escape and died of his injuries
Manfred Weylandt	Age 29	*12.07.1942	†14.02.1972	Shot while trying to escape
Klaus Schulze	Age 18	*13.10.1953	†07.03.1972	Shot while trying to escape
Cengaver Katranci	Age 7/8	*1964	†30.10.1972	Drowned in border waters

1973

Holger H.	Age 1/2	*1971	†22.01.1973	Suffocated during his parents' successful escape attempt
Volker Frommann	Age 28	*23.04.1944	†05.03.1973	Fatally injured while trying to escape
Horst Einsiedel	Age 33	*08.02.1940	†15.03.1973	Shot while trying to escape
Manfred Gertzki	Age 30	*17.05.1942	†27.04.1973	Shot while trying to escape
Siegfried Kroboth	Age 5	*23.04.1968	†14.05.1973	Drowned in border waters

1974

Burkhard Niering	Age 23	*01.09.1950	†05.01.1974	Shot while trying to escape
Johannes Sprenger	Age 68	*03.12.1905	†10.05.1974	Shot while trying to escape
Giuseppe Savoca	Age 6	*22.04.1968	†15.06.1974	Drowned in border waters

1975

Herbert Halli	Age 21	*24.11.1953	†03.04.1975	Shot while trying to escape
Cetin Mert	Age 5	*11.05.1970	†11.05.1975	Drowned in border waters
Herbert Kiebler	Age 23	*24.03.1952	†27.06.1975	Shot while trying to escape
Lothar Hennig	Age 21	*30.06.1954	†05.11.1975	Shot during a search operation in the border area with no intent to escape

1977

| Dietmar Schwietzer | Age 18 | *21.02.1958 | †16.02.1977 | Shot while trying to escape |
| Henri Weise | Age 22 | *13.07.1954 | †May 1977 | Retrieved dead from the Spree River near the Marschall Bridge |

1980

Marienetta Jirkowsky	Age 18	*25. 08. 1962	† 22. 11. 1980	Shot while trying to escape
Peter Grohganz	Age 32	*25. 09. 1948	† Dec. 1980	Drowned while trying to escape

1981

Dr. Johannes Muschol	Age 31	*31. 05. 1949	† 16. 03. 1981	West German shot in the border area
Hans-Jürgen Starrost	Age 25	*24. 06. 1955	† 16. 05. 1981	Shot at while trying to escape and died of his injuries
Thomas Taubmann	Age 26	*22. 07. 1955	† 12. 12. 1981	Fatally injured while trying to escape

1982

Lothar Fritz Freie	Age 27	*08. 02. 1955	† 06. 06. 1982	West Berliner shot in the border area

1983

Silvio Proksch	Age 21	*03. 03. 1962	† 25. 12. 1983	Shot while trying to escape

1984

Michael Schmidt	Age 20	*20. 10. 1964	† 01. 12. 1984	Shot while trying to escape

1986

Rainer Liebeke	Age 34	*11. 09. 1951	† 03. 09. 1986	Drowned while trying to escape
René Gross	Age 22	*01. 05. 1964	† 21. 11. 1986	Shot while trying to escape
Manfred Mäder	Age 38	*23. 08. 1948	† 21. 11. 1986	Shot while trying to escape
Michael Bittner	Age 25	*31. 08. 1961	† 24. 11. 1986	Shot while trying to escape

1987

Lutz Schmidt	Age 24	*08. 07. 1962	† 12. 02. 1987	Shot while trying to escape

1989

Ingolf Diederichs	Age 24	*13. 04. 1964	† 13. 01. 1989	Fatally injured while trying to escape
Chris Gueffroy	Age 20	*21. 06. 1968	† 05. 02. 1989	Shot while trying to escape
Winfried Freudenberg	Age 32	*29. 08. 1956	† 08. 03. 1989	Fatally injured while trying to escape in a balloon

East German border soldiers who were killed by military deserters, fellow soldiers, fugitives, an escape helper or a West Berlin policeman while on duty

1962

Jörgen Schmidtchen	Age 20	*28.06.1941	† 18.04.1962	Shot by an NVA officer cadet who was also killed
Peter Göring	Age 21	*28.12.1940	† 23.05.1962	Fatally injured by a ricochet bullet fired by a West Berlin policeman
Reinhold Huhn	Age 20	*08.03.1942	† 18.06.1962	Shot by a West Berlin escape helper
Günter Seling	Age 22	*28.04.1940	† 30.09.1962	Accidentally shot by an East German border soldier

1963

Siegfried Widera	Age 22	*12.02.1941	† 08.09.1963	Died of injuries after being knocked out by fugitives

1964

Egon Schultz	Age 21	*04.01.1943	† 05.10.1964	Accidentally shot by an East German border soldier

1968

Rolf Henniger	Age 26	*30.11.1941	† 15.11.1968	Shot by an East German policeman who had deserted and was also killed

1980

Ulrich Steinhauer	Age 24	*13.03.1956	† 04.11.1980	Shot by a border soldier who had deserted

8
The Wall
in the Honecker Era
(1971–1989)

The Wall in the Honecker Era

For a long time during the Honecker era, the GDR seems economically and politically stable. But appearances are deceptive. The economy is ailing. The Soviet superpower is entering a crisis. The East German communist regime commits itself to respecting human rights as the price for its international recognition, and more and more people want to hold it to this commitment – particularly those wanting to leave the country.

At the beginning of the Honecker era, there is a huge programme to improve social welfare and consumer opportunities, designed to keep the people quiet. The DDR does not want to see a revolt like the one in Prague in 1968 or workers' protests like those in Poland in 1970 happening on its soil.

After the Eighth SED Party Congress in April 1971, wages and pensions are raised. The number of holidays is increased. Fulltime working mothers receive social benefits. New housing is built; rents remain low. The prices for basic foodstuffs are frozen, as are those for energy consumption and public transport. While West Germany is drawn into the world recession in 1974/75 and confronted with unemployment, the GDR seems to being catching up economically; a modest degree of prosperity begins to spread.

At the start of the 1970s, on the basis of the Four-Power Agreement on Berlin, both German states agree, in numerous ensuing pacts, to make it easier to travel from West to East, to open new border crossings and to improve the connections by road and rail as well as postal and telephone communications. From 3 October 1972, after years of division, the West Berliners are given the chance to visit the GDR, including East Berlin, once or several times a year for up to thirty days, for "humanitarian, family, religious, cultural or tourism" reasons. The city stops growing apart: up to the end of 1989, West Berliners undertake 44 million trips to the GDR and East Berlin.

< Previous page: Death strip between Berlin-Mitte and Wedding (Bernauer Strasse), late 1980s.

"Erich, let me tell you quite frankly,
never forget this:
the GDR cannot exist without us,
without the Soviet Union,
its power and strength.
Without us there is no GDR. [...]
There must not be
any process of rapprochement
between the FRG and the GDR."

Remark from CPSU General Secretary Leonid Brezhnev to Erich Honecker, Ulbricht's designated successor, 28 July 1970.

In December 1972, West Germany and East Germany sign the "Basic Treaty", which is meant to lead to "normal and neighbourly relations" on the basis of equality. West Germany recognises the GDR as an independent state and accepts the inviolability of its border. Differences in opinion, for example on the national question, are put aside.

The German-German treaty policy ends East Germany's political isolation. The international recognition of the GDR reaches its zenith with the country's acceptance into the United Nations and its participation at the Conference on Security and Cooperation in Europe (CSCE) in Helsinki – together with West Germany. On 1 August 1975, the GDR, together with 34 other nations, signs the "Helsinki Accords", in which the participating states commit themselves to the renunciation of violence, the inviolability of borders and non-intervention in the internal affairs of other countries in Europe, as well as to respecting human rights and basic freedoms. The document also affirms the right to freely choose one's place of residence.

Concrete and hard currency

The international recognition of the East German communist regime boosts its confidence. The financial benefits that it receives from West Germany for "humanitarian relief" fill its coffers with foreign currency. Transit, postal and visa fees, renovating the motorway and additional border crossings, the compulsory exchange of currency when visiting the GDR – all of this flushes billons of DM into the GDR. Increasingly the Wall turns into an abundant source of foreign currency. Between 1975 and 1979, the income from West Germany for "humanitarian concessions" climbs from almost 600 million DM to 1.56 billion DM and remains at this high level during the ensuing years. The income from the ransom of prisoners doubles in comparison with the 1960s; from 1975 it comes to between 100 and 200 million DM annually, and even more in peak years.

Although the SED leadership would not want to do without these sources of income, it fears the ideological subversion of the population through visits and packages from the West and not least through Western media, which bring a more attractive consumer world, free thought and uncensored news to the GDR. Unnoticed by the public, the détente triggers an expansion of the Ministry for State Security into a comprehensive surveillance apparatus. Between 1970 and 1980, the number of Stasi employees doubles from around 40,000 to around 80,000.

In 1972, as a particularly "neighbourly" act, Erich Honecker orders new mines (SM-70) to be introduced on the inner-German border. Successfully tested on wild game, the sharp-edged pellets from these electrical self-firing devices can also inflict fatal injuries on humans or wound them so severely that they mostly can no longer get through the border. The self-firing devices are not installed on the Berlin border – for fear that their effect could be documented from the West side.

"Neighbourly relations": splinter mines – filled with 110 grammes of TNT and more than 100 steel cubes – employed against GDR escapees on the inner-German border (early 1980s).

New mines (SM-70)
at the inner-German border:
The self-firing devices
are not installed
on the Berlin border –
for fear that their brutal effect
could be documented
from the West side.

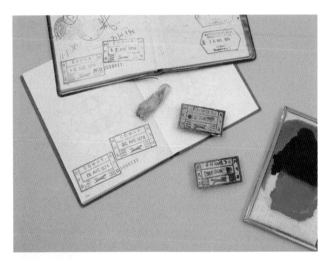

Any hopes the East Germans may have that they, too, will be able to pass through the Wall more easily towards the West as a result of the German-German détente are at first not fulfilled. With the introduction of passport- and visa-free travel to Poland and Czechoslovakia, the SED leaders only open a valve for travelling to the East.

From 1964, only pensioners, who are no longer of use to the economy, are allowed to take trips to the West. In 1972, GDR citizens below retirement age are given the opportunity to visit their relatives in the West for "urgent family reasons"; however, the approved reasons for travel are limited to births, marriages, important wedding anniversaries and deaths of first-degree West German relatives. Applicants have to have their employer's written permission and relatives, especially children, who have to be left in the GDR as hostages. Up to 1982, only 40,000 citizens per year are given permission to visit their relatives in the Federal Republic.

Helping escapees with forged visas: imitation Bulgarian entry and exit stamps are hand-made to help people escape with doctored West German passports.

In view of the prospect of only being able to leave the GDR as a pensioner, many people continue to try to escape. Escape aid, which has become increasingly professional – and also more commercial – is given a temporary boost by the transit agreement.

But with more and more comprehensive surveillance of transit routes, the infiltration of escape-aid groups by informers and, at the start of the 1980s, even assassination attempts on escape helpers, the secret police manages to curb organised escape assistance.

Helped 33 people escape – Hartmut Richter, sentenced to 15 years in jail for providing "escape assistance" in 1975, ransomed by West Germany in 1980

In January 1966, 18-year-old Hartmut Richter tries to reach the West via the Czech-Austrian border. But his attempt fails. Richter, who does not accept the SED regime, is arrested and given a suspended ten-month prison sentence by the Potsdam District Court in May 1966. Another escape attempt at the end of August 1966 is successful: Hartmut Richter swims through the Teltow Canal in the district of Dreilinden to West Berlin.

His escape experience has a profound influence on him. Up until 1972, Harmut Richter travels the world as a ship's steward. When he returns to West Berlin, the transit agreement between West Germany and East Germany comes into force. It makes it easier to hide escapees from the GDR in West German vehicles and bring them to the West on the transit routes. In the same year, the "illegal emigrant" ("Republikflüchtling") Hartmut Richter is allowed to travel to the GDR again under an amnesty.

In 1973, an acquaintance asks him to find a suitable escape helper for a female friend from the GDR. Hartmut Richter decides to assist in the escape attempt himself. His former home village in the GDR, Glindow, is situated directly next to the transit motorway Berlin-Hanover. The would-be escapee is to wait for him in a shed on his parents' property, where he will pick her up and take her to West Berlin in the boot of his car. The plan works, and the woman succeeds in escaping.

This first escape is followed by others. Soon, Hartmut Richter, who has now started to study, realises that his client sees helping people to escape as a business and earns money from it. In principle, he does not think this is objectionable, as preparing an escape requires a lot of time and there is great risk involved for the escape agent. But the amounts of money demanded seem disproportionately high, and he does not take on any more jobs. Instead, Hartmut Richter helps friends and acquaintances to escape from the GDR independently. He picks up the escapees in the tried and tested way in Glindow or at a bus stop near Finkenkrug. With his help, a total of 33 people make it to the West.

In the night of 3-4 March 1975, Hartmut Richter wants to help his sister and her fiancé to escape to West Berlin in the boot of his car. The Stasi suspects Richter, stops the car at the Drewitz border crossing and inspects it. Both escapees and their helper are arrested and detained in the Stasi remand prison in Potsdam.

On 12 December 1975, the Potsdam District Court sentences Hartmut Richter to the maximum period of 15 years in jail for "subversive human trafficking in order to damage the GDR". Just under five years and seven months later, on 2 October 1980, Hartmut Richter is ransomed from the Bautzen II prison and released to the "independent political unit of West Berlin".

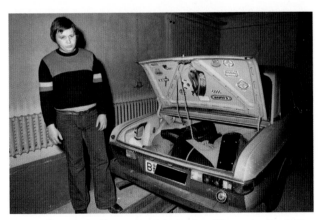

Caught in the act: the Stasi forces escape helpers and would-be escapees to recreate their escape attempt in a garage, 1975.

Ransoming: Reprehensible human trafficking or humanitarian act?

Between 1964 and 1989, in return for concessions to the tune of about 3.5 billion DM, the West German government gains the premature release of 33,755 prisoners, succeeds in bringing 2,000 children over the border to their parents and brings about around 250,000 family reunifications. It is still a matter of controversy whether the ransom of prisoners was a humanitarian act or a reprehensible form of human trafficking.

More than 70,000 people receive escape-related jail sentences between 1960 and 1989. Those who the West buys free are usually transferred to the Stasi remand prison in Karl-Marx-Stadt (Chemnitz) shortly before their release, and taken to the West from there by coach.

Payments by the West German government for the ransom of political prisoners and family reunification from 1964 to 1990

Year	Ransomed political prisoners	Family reunifications	Payment (DM)
1964	884	–	37,918,901.16
1965	1,555	762	67,667,898.52
1966	407	393	24,805,316.38
1967	554	438	31,482,433.19
1968	693	405	28,435,444.15
1969	880	408	44,873,875.05
1970	888	595	50,589,774.55
1971	1,375	911	84,223,481.52
1972*	731	1,219	69,457,704.26
1973	631	1,124	54,028,288.39
1974	1,053	2,450	88,147,719.74
1975	1,158	5,635	104,012,504.93
1976	1,439	4,734	30,003,535.00
1977	1,475	2,886	143,997,942.27
1978	1,452	3,979	168,363,141.86
1979	890	4,205	106,986,866.24
1980	1,036	3,931	130,015,131.77
1981	1,584	7,571	178,987,210.84
1982	1,491	6,304	176,999,590.94
1983	1,105	5,487	102,811,953.50
1984	2,236	29,626	387,997,305.12
1985	2,669	17,315	301,995,568.10
1986	1,450	15,767	195,009,307.73
1987	1,209	8,225	162,997,921.59
1988	1,048	21,202	232,096,191.43
1989	1,775	69,447	267,895,657.76
1990	–	–	65,000,089.13
Total	**33,755**	**215,019**	**3,436,800,755.12**

* In 1972, a further 2,087 prisoners are released to the West under a GDR amnesty.

The second Cold War

At the end of the 1970s, East-West relations worsen – a second Cold War sets in. It is triggered by the stationing of Soviet medium-range atomic missiles in Europe. In response, NATO reacts with a double resolution at the end of 1979: it offers the Warsaw Pact nations disarmament talks – and at the same time announces that, if they break down, it will also install medium-range nuclear missiles in West Germany, Great Britain and Italy from the end of 1983. The Soviet invasion of Afghanistan in December 1979, the imposition of martial law in Poland in December 1981 and the shooting down of a civilian passenger aircraft belonging to Korean Airlines by Soviet interceptors at the end of August 1983 contribute to making the climate even more tense. In 1983, US President Ronald Reagan calls the Soviet Union the "evil empire" – and announces a "Strategic Defence Initiative" (SDI). The research programme, costing billions of dollars, for a space-based non-nuclear missile defence system is intended to force the Soviet Union to its knees both militarily and financially. When the West German parliament approves the stationing of American medium-range missiles in December 1983, the Soviet leadership breaks off all international disarmament talks. East-West relations deteriorate to freezing point.

During this period, both German states try to dissociate inner-German relations from the growing international tensions. There is a common motive for this: the fear of a nuclear conflict, which threatens above all both East and West Germany with atomic destruction – irrespective of their different political systems. Moreover, West Germany does not want to risk the "humanitarian concessions" that it has wrung – and bought – from the GDR in the past years. For the GDR, on the other hand, its existence is already at stake: the consumer socialism of the 1970s is based on credit. A growth in military spending, a cessation of loans from the West and the tightening of embargo measures make its already precarious economic situation worse – like that of all other Eastern Bloc countries as well. In 1981, the GDR – along with Poland, Hungary and Romania – is on the brink of not being able to repay its heavy debts with the West.

"From Stettin on the Baltic to Varna on the Black Sea, the regimes planted by totalitarianism have had more than 30 years to establish their legitimacy. But none – not one regime – has yet been able to risk free elections. Regimes planted by bayonets do not take root." President Ronald Reagan, Speech to the House of Commons, 8 June 1982.

"The USA is aiming for a kind of 'crusade' against the socialist community. [...] There has never been a US administration as unrestrained and aggressive as Reagan's." Conversation between Leonid Brezhnev and Erich Honecker, 11 August 1982.

The GDR is threatened with insolvency in the first quarter of 1982.

Secret Stasi report, 25 January 1982.

The continued flow of hard currency from West Germany is thus vital for the SED leadership. No help is to be expected from the Soviet Union; on the contrary, the Soviet Union at first stops delivering grain to the GDR, then reduces the supply of oil and refuses to give the GDR any further loans – and finally even demands financial support for Poland – and itself. In 1981/82, the Soviet Union is also in a deep economic crisis. For this reason, Erich Honecker and his Central Committee Economics Secretary Günter Mittag pull back from the total collision course with West Germany that a critically ill Brezhnev again calls for in the summer of 1982.

And they are rewarded: with two loans of a billion DM from West Germany in 1983 and 1984 and a third billion concealed in the form of ransoms and postal fees, the GDR manages to avert the imminent economic collapse and the internal unrest that would likely have resulted, and to temporarily stabilise the country.

The political price that the SED leadership is willing to pay for this – at a later date, so that the direct connection is not evident – is considerable. It not only removes the mines from the inner-German border, but also makes the Wall more passable, also allowing a growing number of visits to the West by GDR citizens. In addition, in a unique action in 1984, almost all applications for permanent departure to West Germany are approved.

German-German "coalition of reason" despite a new international ice age: Meeting between West German chancellor Helmut Schmidt and East German communist party leader Erich Honecker on Werbellin Lake in the GDR, 11 – 13 December 1981.

The emigration movement

From the mid-1970s, between 8,000 and 15,000 people apply to leave the GDR permanently every year. They cannot claim any legal basis, but refer instead to the CSCE Helsinki Accords and other human rights conventions that obligate the GDR, like other countries, to respect human rights. These include "freedom of movement" – the right to leave one's country and return again.

But those wanting to leave are mostly discriminated against and criminalised. Anyone who applies for permission to leave and continues to try despite rejection by the GDR authorities "impedes" the "state and social activity" (GDR Penal Code § 214). Anyone who seeks assistance from the West – from relatives, friends or state institutions – is guilty of "illegal contact" (GDR Penal Code § 219) or even "traitorous information transfer or activities as an agent" (GDR Penal Code §§ 99, 100). Anyone who criticises the political situation in the GDR to lend more weight to his/her intention to leave is accused of "public disparagement" (GDR Penal Code, § 220). Up until 1989, the State Security arrests well over 10,000 people for offences against these paragraphs of the penal code.

In 1983 – after the follow-up CSCE meeting in Madrid – the GDR Council of Ministers for the first time issues a regulation that, in a purely formal sense, gives citizens the right to apply to "move the place of [their] residence abroad", but limits this to people wanting to move to first-degree relatives and spouses. By far the majority of the now more than 30,000 applicants does not fall into this category. In many places, people wanting to leave the GDR join to form groups; at the start of 1984, others occupy the United States Embassy and the West German Permanent Mission in East Berlin. The media in the West take up the subject – the SED leadership comes under pressure. This fact – and the loans amounting to billions from West Germany – causes the SED leadership to allow more than 20,000 applicants to move to the West in the spring of 1984.

But any hope that this will mean a permanent end to its emigration problems is not fulfilled. Instead, this approval of applications on a mass scale has an avalanche effect. The number of applications to leave the GDR increases by leaps and bounds – to more than 70,000 by the end of 1986 and to more than 100,000 the year after that.

As the applicants' dissatisfaction with the restrictive treatment of these "requests to move" grows, so does their readiness to hold organised and public protests. In Dresden, 300 would-be emigrants demonstrate with the motto: "Erich, give us the key!" In Leipzig, hundreds of youths draw attention to the violation of their basic right during the Spring Trade Fair. In many places, prayer ceremonies for peace and services of intercession in churches become the starting point for protest actions against the denial of people's right to leave the country.

In 1988, the State Security suggests taking action against the would-be emigrants with "resolution and all due severity"; it says the groups should be broken up and their initiators arrested and sentenced. The Stasi advises strongly against any new rise in approving applications, saying this would give the "enemies" a boost and attract still more applicants.

But Honecker disregards these suggestions: he opens the departure valve. In April 1988, he gives the order to increase the number of applications approved per month from 1,000 to 2,000–3,000. Yet again, his strategy does not work: the number of applicants increases. In the first half of 1989, the SED Secretary-General goes further, allowing 6,000 departures per month. "This has gone far enough!" he cries, unnerved, on 5 July 1989 – but the number of applications reaches the record level of 125,400.

Neither by approving applications nor by imposing disciplinary, discriminatory and openly repressive measures does the SED leadership succeed in winning the fight against people's desire to leave the country. A constantly growing number of people is ready to put up with years of persecution or even prison sentences to be able to travel to West Germany.

Applicants for permanent departure from the GDR 1977 – 1989*

Year	Applicants (Total/First Time) (31.12. / per year)	Applications (Revoked / Permitted) (per year /Total)
1977	– / 8,400	800 / 2,500
1978	– / 5,400	700 / 3,700
1979	– / 7,700	4,300 / 4,500
1980	21,500 / 9,800	4,700 / 3,600
1981	23,000 / 12,300	5,000 / 7,600
1982	24,900 / 13,500	6,500 / 6,300
1983	30,300 / 14,800	5,600 / 5,600
1984	50,600 / 57,600	17,300 / 27,500
1985	53,000 / 27,300	11,300 / 14,700
1986	78,600 / 50,600	10,800 / 14,500
1987	105,100 / 43,200	12,800 / 6,300
1988	113,500 / 42,400	11,700 / 24,200
1989**	125,400 / 23,000	1,400 / 36,600

* Columns rounded off to nearest hundred. ** (30.6.)

"Clarification of circumstances" – Gisela Lotz, sentenced to imprisonment with her entire family in 1985 for applications to leave the country, ransomed by West Germany in 1986.

Gisela and Kurt Lotz in the year they applied to leave the GDR, 1982.

When her parents flee to the West in the early summer of 1961, Gisela Lotz is 18 years old. Lotz, a trained gardener, promises to follow soon. But she is unable to keep her word – the building of the Wall on 13 August prevents her.

Gisela Lotz marries, starts a family and builds a house near Potsdam. She tries to gain permission to visit her parents in Pforzheim again and again, without success.

In February 1982, Gisela Lotz, her husband and her two grown-up sons apply for family reunification and migration to West Germany. The application is rejected, and 13 further applications as well. Lotz's father turns to institutions in West Germany for assistance. Father and daughter inform one another of their efforts in their letters.

In the morning of 15 August 1985, the doorbell rings at the home of Kurt and Gisela Lotz. Two men ask them to come along to "clarify circumstances". Thinking that the visit concerns their exit permit, the couple allow themselves to be taken to Potsdam. The trip ends in the Stasi remand prison. Only after hours of interrogation does Gisela Lotz realise that she has been arrested along with her husband – and her two sons as well, as she learns in the evening.

On 23 December 1985, the family comes before the court behind closed doors. It is the first time they have seen one another since they were arrested;

Cell ("tiger cage") in the Potsdam Stasi remand prison, Lindenstrasse 54/55.

they are not permitted to embrace or shake hands. The court sentences Kurt and Gisela Lotz to two years and four months in prison for "illegal contacts" (Paragraph 219 of the GDR Penal Code). One son is sentenced to one year and eight months in prison, the other to one year and sixth months. The men have to serve their sentences in different prisons, while Gisela Lotz is taken to Hoheneck women's prison.

On 4 November 1986, after more than 14 months in jail, Gisela Lotz, her husband and one of their sons are allowed to leave the GDR – ransomed by West Germany. Four weeks later, their second son is permitted to follow them to Pforzheim.

Border crossing points

The various tasks at the border crossing points are divided up between border troops, Stasi officials and customs officers. The border troops are in charge of military security, particularly the prevention of border break-throughs. But they only nominally provide the "commander" of the border crossing, as the matter of cross-border traffic is too important to the SED regime for it to leave it up to the border troops, which are made up of conscripts and thus constantly changing. For this reason, the security, control and surveillance of the entire cross-border traffic, including both searches and arrests, are the province of passport control units from the secret police, albeit disguised in the uniform of the border troops.

The customs carry out the inspection of goods and people. The People's Police are not directly present at the border crossing, but have the task of keeping the area just before it, the so-called "freundwärtiges Hinter-land" ("friend-wards hinterland"), clear of anything that could disturb the flow of traffic. Owing to the numerous attempts at escape, the border crossings are gradually extended into long fortifications protected by concrete and steel, secured against both fast runners and attempts to break through using heavy equipment.

"I want out! Without escaping": Protester on the Eastern side of Bornholmer Strasse border crossing, 7 October 1988.

Harald Jäger, lieutenant-colonel, deputy head of the Ministry for State Security passport inspection unit at the Bornholmer Strasse border crossing "Every day, GDR citizens came to us who said simply: 'We want to go across!' Mostly at night. People came with their children and said simply that they wanted to leave – without a visa or anything else. The attempt was not really a criminal offence but just an infringement. At first we reprimanded them and sent them back; later, we had to arrest them for attempted illegal border crossing under § 213 of the Penal Code."

The "Palace of Tears" – inspection building for passport and customs processing at Friedrichstrasse Station.

Border railway station Friedrichstrasse

From 13 August 1961, the Friedrichstrasse railway station becomes a border railway station – in the middle of East Berlin. Only the entrance hall and the overground platform "C" are accessible to normal GDR citizens. Walls and screens cut this platform off from the northern platforms "A" and "B", to which only travellers from the West have access – as is also the case with the underground north-south train lines. To get to these, travellers have to go through a building in which passport and customs inspections take place: the so-called "Palace of Tears", where visitors from the West have to say farewell to their relatives and friends from the East. The Friedrichstrasse Railway Station provides the GDR with ideal conditions for infiltrating and retrieving agents. West Berliners, for their part, like to use the GDR Intershops when disembarking and changing trains to stock up on duty-free cigarettes and spirits – thus helping the GDR to obtain vital hard currency.

Wall of surveillance monitors in the observation headquarters at Friedrichstrasse Station – over 100 TV cameras film every nook and cranny.

In the inspection traps, pictures of passports are sent via video to the records room. There, officers compare the data by hand with the wanted persons files: an automatically collated card index covering some 60–70,000 people.

Border crossing Bornholmer Strasse

Harald Jäger, lieutenant-colonel, deputy head of the Ministry for State Security passport inspection unit at the Bornholmer Strasse border crossing "In the case of West Berliners or West German citizens, you have to learn to tell whether it is someone who is really hostile towards us, or whether he only wants to enter the country to get to know it and its people or just to visit his relatives. And the 'negative' people and the 'hostile' ones: we have to find out who they are. After all, no one had it written on their face that they were an enemy of the GDR.

We tried to strike up conversations with the people entering the country. On the one hand, we wanted to know what was going on over there, and on the other we wanted to find out something about them. Some liked to talk and spoke with us. There were also some who liked us.

As far as the GDR citizens were concerned who travelled to the Western part, they were mostly only pensioners. They went across because of the supply situation in the GDR: we were aware of that. And it was also clear to us that young GDR citizens were not allowed to travel. Firstly, there was no Western money. Our currency couldn't be exchanged and we as a state didn't have the money to allow everyone to travel. So it was an economic necessity for us that they weren't allowed to travel."

The Bornholmer Strasse border crossing point is in the densely populated East Berlin borough of Prenzlauer Berg. The local people, mainly workers, live in tenement buildings right up to the border crossing and the barrier facilities.

Border crossing Glienicke Bridge

The Glienecke Bridge connects Berlin and Potsdam. Its eastern part is in the West and its western part in the East; the border runs through the middle of the bridge. After 1961, it can be used as a border crossing point only by Allied military personnel or with special permission. Glienicke Bridge gains worldwide fame because of an exchange of agents between the USA and the Soviet Union: on 10 February 1962, the US pilot Gary Powers is exchanged for the top Soviet spy, Rudolf Ivanovitch Abel. Powers had been shot down over the Soviet Union in a U2 spy plane on 1 May 1960; Abel had spied for the Soviet Union for nine years in New York when he was arrested in 1957. On 12 June 1985, 23 agents from the West and four agents from the East cross over the bridge in opposite directions. On 11 February 1986, the Soviet human rights activist, Anatoli Sharansky, and three spies held in the GDR or Czechoslovakia are received on the Western side; in exchange, five agents from Czechoslovakia, Poland and the Soviet Union who have been detained in the West cross the bridge towards the GDR.

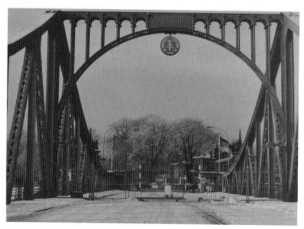

Border crossing Glienicke Bridge, seen from West Berlin, 1980s.

Border crossing point only for Allied military personell and since 1985 for diplomats: Glienicke Bridge between West Berlin and Potsdam. < East / West >

Climax of the Cold War: The body of US Major Arthur D. Nicholson is transported to West Berlin over Glienicke Bridge on 25 March 1985. According to US officials, he was on an official trip from Berlin to Hamburg; Soviet officials say Nicholson was shot dead while he was photographing Soviet military facilities.

Concealed gamma ray devices at East Berlin border crossings

From 1979/80, radioactive rays are used to look for escapees at all border crossings. Cars and trucks are screened using hidden gamma-ray devices. These are connected with electronic computers and produce a screen image showing passengers – and concealed people – as shadows.

After 1990, there is heated discussion about whether the rays endangered or harmed people. The Federal Radiation Protection Commission comes to the conclusion that, although the methods used by the GDR authorities contravened basic guidelines on radiation protection, the screenings did not produce "a harmful dose".

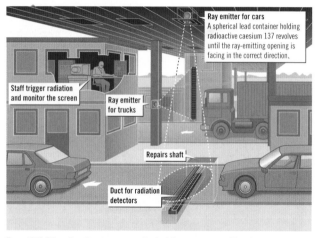

Ray emitter for cars
A spherical lead container holding radioactive caesium 137 revolves until the ray-emitting opening is facing in the correct direction.

Staff trigger radiation and monitor the screen

Ray emitter for trucks

Repairs shaft

Duct for radiation detectors

From 1979/80, radioactive rays are used to look for escapees at all border crossings.

Escapes in the 1980s

By the 1980s the web of surveillance and spying is so dense that over 90 percent of the 1,000 to 2,000 escape plans every year are betrayed and prevented at the planning stage. Only five to eight percent of escape attempts are successful.

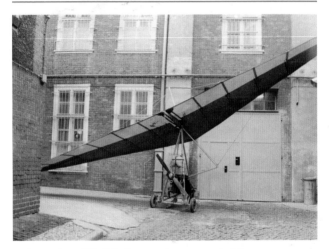

20 December 1986: Failed escape in a powered glider

In the evening of 20 December 1986, a 37-year-old hang-gliding enthusiast launches an escape attempt near Potsdam in a home-made, motor-driven glider. Poor visibility, difficulty in getting his bearings and the cold force the man, a toolmaker, to land – back on GDR soil. He is arrested on the basis of information provided by residents from several areas who observed the flight.

The glider is assembled in the yard of the Potsdam Stasi prison and photographed as "evidence".

15 July 1987: Successful escape in a light plane

On his second solo flight, the 18-year-old Thomas K. flies beneath all radar detection to land at the British military airfield in West Berlin. His motive: "dissatifaction with the political system in the GDR"; he wants to join his relatives in the Federal Republic. British military personnel hand over the disassembled single-engine plane to the GDR on 5 August 1987 at Glienicke Bridge.

9 December 1987: Failed escape by car on Glienicke Bridge

On 9 December 1987, 22-year-old Axel D. and 27-year-old Bernd S. try to break through the barriers on Glienicke Bridge in a "Wolga M 21" car. Bernd S. has put in an unsuccessful application to leave the GDR. The car crashes into the closed entrance gate to the lane used by the military and detaches it from its hinges. It then skids into the gatepost, coming to a halt at the very first obstacle. Axel D. and Bernd S. are arrested.

10 March 1988: First successful escape over Glienicke Bridge

Driving in a truck, three young men – Gotthard Ihden, Bernd Puhlmann and Werner Jäger – make the first successful escape over Glienecke Bridge. The 7.5-tonne truck, disguised as a "dangerous goods transport" and loaded with 92 empty gas canisters, breaks through four obstacles: the entrance gate, a swing-arm barrier, a drop-arm barrier and a steel gate. No shots are fired. "I did it for love," says one of the escapees, who is following his wife to the West. "It was not an adventure for me, but a suicide mission. I had given myself only a five-percent chance of survival."

Failed escape attempt in a Skoda car at the Mahlow border crossing to Berlin-Lichtenrade, 29 June 1989

Shortly before 10 p.m. on 29 June 1989, a 27-year-old electrician from Wiederau in Brandenburg makes an escape attempt. He approaches the Mahlow border crossing in his Skoda car, observing the regulations by driving at walking speed with his lights dimmed.

Then he accelerates and breaks through the first toll bar. The border soldiers trigger the alarm and close all the barriers. The driver nevertheless manages to drive through two more toll bars before crashing into a barrier at 70 kilometres an hour.

The front of the car is wrecked. The severely injured driver is taken to the Postdam army hospital and handed over to the local Stasi.

Gorbachev and Reagan – Honecker and Kohl

The freeze in relations between the Soviet Union and the USA ends when Mikhail Gorbachev comes to power in March 1985 as the Secretary-General of the CPSU. The Soviet Union is in the midst of a severe economic and social crisis. Gorbachev's new foreign policies are geared towards reducing conflict and stopping the arms race in a bid to limit Soviet military spending. He is convinced that the politics of renewal he has introduced in the Soviet Union ("perestroika") have little chance of success unless the burden of military expenditure is reduced.

At first, the Reagan administration is sceptical about whether Gorbachev really differs from his predecessors in anything more than age. But after a short while, US-Soviet disarmament talks gather momentum. At only their second meeting, in Reykjavik in 1986, Reagan and Gorbachev already discuss removing all medium-range atomic missiles from Europe and even largely abolishing all nuclear weapons, albeit without yet reaching any agreement. In December 1987, both state leaders finally sign a pact on removing the intermediate-range missiles (INF) within three years. Reagan makes the ratification of this pact dependent on the Soviet withdrawal from Afghanistan. In 1990, the US president describes his relationship with Gorbachev as a "friendship between two men".

In Moscow and Washington, the special path taken by the two Germanies during the second Cold War has led to doubts about the reliability of each respective German ally. In 1987, for example, the Reagan administration shows concern about the two Germanies' policy of rapprochement. It obviously thinks the West Germans are capable of coming to terms with the Wall permanently in return for small concessions, for example with regard to travel, letting go of basic principles such as the four-power status of Berlin, moral concepts of freedom and even reunification. A state visit by Erich Honecker in Bonn is scheduled for September 1987, and the Mayor of Berlin, Eberhard Diepgen, has even invited the SED Secretary-

General to West Berlin for the city's 750th anniversary. In February 1987 – as once before at the end of 1986 – the Senate is noticeably reticent in its protests against fatal shootings at the Wall – possibly so as not to endanger its policy of invitations. In March 1987, it is American authorities that inform the public that a would-be escapee from the GDR has been shot trying to flee to West Berlin: 24-year-old Lutz Schmidt. Ahead of Reagan's visit to Berlin, Washington warns the city's mayor not to be too "soft" towards the Soviet Union and the GDR.

"[East] Berlin could be tempted to throw itself into the arms of West Germany under the pressure of economic problems."

Mikhail Gorbachev at a meeting of the CPSU politburo, 27 March 1986.

Gorbachev, on the other hand, does not trust Erich Honecker. On 27 March 1986, he tells the CPSU Polibüro that "[East] Berlin could be tempted to throw itself into the arms of West Germany under the pressure of economic problems."

The SED Secretary-General dissociates himself from the politics of "perestroika", at first covertly, then more and more openly. He feels that reforms in the GDR are superfluous, and sees them more as a danger for socialism than anything else.

Four statesmen – five meetings: a sixth meeting – Erich Honecker's dream – is never to take place. Left: Reagan (USA) and Gorbachev (USSR), October 1986; Kohl (West Germany) and Reagan, June 1987; Honecker (East Germany) and Kohl, September 1987.
Top: Kohl and Gorbachev, June 1989; Gorbachev and Honecker, October 1989.

Gorbachev still does not show his mistrust publicly. While visiting the border installations at the Brandenburg Gate in April 1986, he writes in the guest book: "At the Brandenburg Gate, one can clearly see how much strength and true heroism the defence of the first socialist state on German soil requires against the attacks of the class enemy." But in one-on-one conversations, Gorbachev voices criticism of Honecker's "certain reserve" towards the Soviet course of reform and even complains that the GDR is keeping many things secret from the Soviet Union – above all its debts to the West.

What disturbs Honecker the most are the new principles for cooperation in the Warsaw Pact, which Gorbachev announces at the end of 1986: "Independence of each party, its right to take sovereign decisions about the development problems in its country, its responsibility to its own people." This means the end of the Brezhnev doctrine, under which the Soviet Union reserved the right to military intervention if it saw socialism threatened in one of the allied Eastern Bloc states. The SED leadership can no longer bank on the support of Soviet tanks if its power is called into question. Honecker feels himself and the GDR are increasingly betrayed by the supreme power. His relationship to Gorbachev becomes increasingly tense.

From 7 to 11 September 1987, Honecker visits West Germany and is received with all the honour due to a head of state. The political recognition of the GDR would seem to have reached its zenith. But the visit to the West does not bring a breakthrough for the SED leadership or for the people of the GDR. Honecker has to listen on – with stony demeanour – as West German Chancellor Helmut Kohl and the Bavarian Prime Minister Franz Josef Strauss criticise the violation of human rights in the GDR, particularly the "order to shoot". The SED leader does not indicate any imminent changes in the GDR.

See also: www.chronik-der-mauer.de > English > 1987 > 7–11 September

"It is evident, for example, that force and the threat of force can no longer be, and should not be instruments of foreign policy. […] The compelling necessity of the principle of freedom of choice is also clear to us. […] Freedom of choice is a universal principle to which there should be no exceptions."

Mikhail Gorbachev, speech at the 43rd U.N. General Assembly Session in New York, 7 December 1988.

After the meeting, Bonn reduces relations with East Berlin to the diplomatically necessary and, above all, non-committal. The turnover in inner-German trade decreases. Only human business continues to flourish: the West German government responds to further measures to make travel to the West easier for GDR citizens by raising the transit fee from 525 to 860 million DM – for the years 1990 to 1999. The number of trips to the West rises steeply in 1987 and 1988, but every application that is refused – and there are a hundred thousand that are – increases the host of unsatisfied people in the GDR. In retrospect, the two years up to 1989 reveal a profound change: German-German relations stagnate and the rift between East Berlin and Moscow deepens, but the relationship of the Soviet Union to the USA and West Germany improves decisively.

"Eternal remembrance of the border soldiers who have given their lives for the socialist GDR."

Michail Gorbachev at the Brandenburg Gate, 16 April 1986. Eighteen years later, he tells German school pupils: "When I remember the Wall in Berlin, I still feel horror at this construction."

"Mr. Gorbachev, tear down this wall."

Bullet-proof glass and vest, 20,000 hand-picked West Berliners: US President Ronald Reagan at the Brandenburg Gate, 12 June 1987.

In the SED politburo, an apocalyptic mood spreads: 1988 is the year in which the failure of consumer socialism becomes clearly evident to the leaders of the party and the state. To keep the people calm, all capital assets have been used up: whole branches of industry have broken down, old buildings and the infrastructure have decayed, damage to the environment is obvious, the debts to the West have spiralled out of control – but the supply of food and consumer goods is still so inadequate that the Stasi warns of a deteriorating mood among the people. "We must prevent the collapse," Honecker demands in the politburo as early as June 1988. And in November 1988 the Central Committee Economics Secretary, Günter Mittag, prophesies to a small group of ecomics experts: "The way things are going now we'll crash into a tree and be a total write-off!"

"The Wall will [...] remain as long as the conditions that led to its construction are not changed. It will still exist in 50 or even 100 years."

"It is necessary to protect our republic from robbers, not to mention those who would like to disturb the stability and peace of Europe. The protection of borders is the sovereign right of every state, and thus also of the GDR."

Erich Honecker, speech at a meeting of the Thomas Müntzer Committee, 19 January 1989.

9
The Fall of the Wall

The Fall of the Wall

"The Wall will […] remain as long as the conditions that led to its construction are not changed," says Secretary-General Erich Honecker in mid-January 1989; it will "still exist in 50 or even 100 years." But the SED leadership soon learns that these conditions are being increasingly called into question: the pressure to change is growing, both externally and internally.

Gorbachev is giving the Warsaw Pact countries more and more independence. Poland and Hungary are the first to introduce democratic reforms. In January 1989, the Soviet Union and all its allies sign the Vienna CSCE agreement. In it, they commit themselves not only to respect, but to legally guarantee, the right of all individuals to leave and return to their countries.

At the start of 1989, more than 100,000 people in the GDR are waiting for their application to leave the country to be approved; more and more of them also publicly demand their right to leave at protests and demonstrations, as in Leipzig. The number of escape attempts has risen significantly since the previous year, with shots still being fired at defenceless escapees. On February 5, 20-year-old Chris Gueffroy is shot dead while trying to escape over the Berlin Wall. A month later, 32-year-old Winfried Freudenberg crosses the Wall in a home-made hot-air balloon, but crashes to his death in West Berlin. International protests start to show an effect: "It is better to let someone get away than to use firearms in the current political situation," is the slogan issued by Honecker on April 3 – and he secretly revokes the "order to shoot".

< Previous page: Crossing the Wall at Bornholmer Strasse crossing point, 9 November 1989. Right: "Inconceivable for all of us – he was so young. We are mourning in infinite pain and great love for Chris Gueffroy, born 21.6.1968, died 6.2.1989, who passed away through a tragic accident."

Thought the guards were no longer ordered to shoot: Chris Gueffroy, 20 years old, shot dead by border soldiers on 5 February 1989. He was the last escapee to be shot dead at the Berlin Wall.

Für uns alle unfaßbar – er war noch so jung.
Wir trauern in unendlichem Schmerz und voll Liebe um

Chris Gueffroy
geb. am 21. 6. 1968   gest. am 6. 2. 1989

der durch einen tragischen Unglücksfall von uns gegangen ist.

Deine Mutti Karin
und Detlef Prenslow
Dein Bruder Stephan
Deine Omi, Onkel Rainer und alle
Familienangehörigen
Deine Freundin Katrin und ihre Mutter
Deine Freunde Drik, Steffi, Stefan, Alex,
Timmi, Annett, Torsten, Bent, Christian,
Roland, Thomas
und alle, die ihn kannten und liebten

Die Trauerfeier findet am 23. 2. 1989, 14 Uhr, in Berlin-Baumschulenweg statt.

Although the East German authorities did everything in their power to keep the death of Chris Gueffroy a secret, his brother managed to send the eastern paper "Berliner Zeitung" an obituary that was printed on 21 February 1989, making reference to a "tragic accident" that had occurred on 6 February. The western media made the connection between the deceased and the shots fired at the border. Chris Gueffroy was buried on 23 February 1989 at the Baumschulenweg Cemetery in Berlin-Treptow amidst tremendous public sympathy. Well over 100 people paid him the last honors under the watchful eye of the East German secret police. Although the East German secret police imposed massive control measures, a few western correspondents managed to enter East Germany in order to attend the funeral and report on it. That same day a memorial cross in honor of Chris Gueffroy was erected on the West Berlin side of the Teltow Canal in Neukölln. Opposition groups in East Germany publicized the murder of Chris Gueffroy in an "open letter to the population of East Germany." The fact that his murder was still referred to as a "tragic accident" during the funeral sermon was described as a shameful demonstration of just how steeped in lies East Germany was.

8 April 1989: Failed escape at the Chausseestrasse border crossing

On 8 April 1989, five days after the secret repeal of the order to shoot, a Stasi passport inspector shoots at Bert G. and Michael G. to prevent them escaping at the Chausseestrasse crossing point.

The two men are arrested and sentenced to 22 and 20 months' imprisonment. Only then is the Stasi instructed not to shoot at escapees.

"It is better to let someone get away than to use firearms in the current political situation."

This was the slogan issued by Honecker on 3 April 1989 – the "order to shoot" was secretly revoked.

Bert G., one of the two would-be escapees, 1993 "I saw the flash of the gun. It ought to have hit me right between the eyes. It's a miracle I'm still alive. The bullet must have whistled past my head at a hair's breadth."

The first hole in the Wall: Hungarian border soldiers taking down the barbed wire fence to Austria, May 1989.

2 May 1989: Hungary opens it's borders

On 2 May 1989, Hungarian border troops demonstratively begin to dis-- mantle the "Iron Curtain" to Austria. However, GDR citizens trying to escape continue to be arrested and extradited. At the start of the summer holidays, would-be GDR emigrants occupy the West German Permanent Mission in East Berlin and West German embassies in Warsaw, Prague and Budapest; thousands of GDR citizens, mostly young people, go on holiday to Hungary with the intention of not returning to the GDR and travelling to West Germany via Austria. Budapest turns into a refugee camp. On 10 September, the Hungarian government tells the East German leadership it will no longer act as assistant border police. It now opens the border to Austria for GDR citizens as well. Tens of thousands of East Germans leave the country for the West via Austria over the next few weeks. The Soviet Union does nothing – no longer helping the GDR.

See also: www.chronik-der-mauer.de > English > 1989 > May

The reaction: young East German couple on the way to a refugee camp in Budapest, September 1989.

East Germans who want to leave occupy the West German embassy in Prague at the end of September 1989.

30 September and 4 October 1989: more than 10,000 of those who occupied the Prague embassy are transported through GDR territory to West Germany in locked trains.

Mass exodus and mass protest

The mass exodus engenders growing mass protests. On 18 September, there are already hundreds of demonstrators in Leipzig who take to the streets after a prayer for peace in the Church of St. Nicholas. Dissidents who until then have met privately or worked under the protection of the church now dare to found independent political groups such as Neues Forum, Demokratie Jetzt and Demokratischer Aufbruch. Civil rights activists prepare to found a Social Democratic party (SDP) as of 7 October. The Stasi combats the opposition, the SED pretends it does not exist: however, via Western media, the civil rights movement reaches the people with its demands for reform.

With the exodus of GDR citizens via Hungary, the Wall is beginning to crumble, but the SED still has support from Prague. The Czechoslovakian government tightens the controls for GDR citizens on its border to Hungary. As a result, at the end of September about 4,000 GDR citizens camp out in the West German embassy in Prague in a bid to force their way into West Germany. On 30 September, Honecker yields and lets the refugees in the embassy leave.

"We're not shedding a single tear for them."

Neues Deutschland, 2 October 1989.

State ceremony for the 40th anniversary of the GDR, attended by all Warsaw Pact leaders including Mikhail Gorbachev, who is greeted with calls of "Gorbi, help us", East Berlin, 7 October 1989.

The options available to the SED leaders are dwindling to two alternatives: either they introduce political reforms – with an uncertain outcome – or they put up a second "Wall" on the borders to Czechoslovakia and Poland and quell demonstrations with force if necessary. The closure of the border to Czechoslovakia on 3 October 1989 and the violent action taken against demonstrators during the state ceremonies marking the 40th anniversary of the GDR would seem to indicate the second course. On the evening of 9 October 1989, a "Chinese solution" seems imminent in Leipzig. Honecker and Mielke give the order to prevent "mobs" and "riots". But too many people take to the streets. In the end, the state authorities capitulate in the face of 70,000 peaceful demonstrators.

See also: www.chronik-der-mauer.de > English > 1989 > October > 7/8/9

"We are the people!"

9 October 1989: Decision Day ("Tag der Entscheidung") in Leipzig
70,000 people demonstrate peacefully for reforms. Although the East German security authorities plan to prevent the demonstration and its staff have practised dispersing it and arresting the "ringleaders", the state does not intervene. The unexpectedly large number of demonstrators breaks the security organs' will to act. In Halle and in Magdeburg, several thousand people also take part in demonstrations.

The "turn around"

On 17 October 1989, Erich Honecker is brought down in the politburo.

His successor, Egon Krenz, announces a "turn around". The SED leadership's main problem, the economic situation of the GDR, is worsening. Together with Alexander Schalck-Golodkowski, the procurer of hard currency, and three other economists, planning chief Gerhard Schuerer presents an analysis of the financial state of the GDR to the politburo on 31 October. The conclusion: the GDR is heavily in debt to the West and on the brink of bankruptcy. It would be necessary to reduce the standard of living by 25 to 30 percent, but this is considered politically impracticable. The proposed solution: the West German government should be offered the Wall as a last bargaining chip for new loans amounting to 12 to 13 billion DM and enhanced economic cooperation.

On the order of Egon Krenz, Schalck begins negotiations in Bonn on the subject. While the talks are going on, the situation in the GDR becomes explosive. Demonstrations against the SED spread throughout the country and reach even the small towns. Hundreds of thousands of people demand free elections, the authorisation of opposition groups and freedom to travel.

When Egon Krenz came to power, he promised to have a new travel law drawn up. But the State Security puts a brake on this. It is afraid that hundreds of thousands will then leave the GDR. And the Planning Commission objects, because there is no money to provide travellers with foreign currency. The result is a bill that limits the permissible duration of travel to thirty days per year in all. It contains "reasons for refusal" that are not clearly defined or verifiable and leave much room for arbitrary decisions. Published on 6 November, the bill leads to even more vehement protests.

The second hole in the Wall: exit from Czechoslovakia requires only an ID card as of 4 November 1989 – queue of Trabis with East Germans wanting to leave on the Czecho-slovakian-Bavarian border, 5 November 1989.

Threats of strike action in the southern districts have caused the SED leader-ship to lift the ban on travel to Czechoslovakia as of 1 November. Immediately, the West German embassy in Prague is again filled with GDR citizens wanting to leave. The inner city of Prague resembles a transit camp for East Germans. Under the pressure of the Czechoslovakian government, the SED politburo decides to allow GDR citizens to leave for West Germany via Czechoslovakia as of 4 November. The Wall is now open not only via the detour through Hungary, but also through neighbouring Czechoslovakia. Within a few days, 50,000 GDR citizens make use of this new route. The Czechoslovakian government protests sharply in East Berlin against the mass migration through its country and formally requests the SED to regulate the emigration of GDR citizens to West Germany directly and not via Czechoslovakian territory.

Demonstration in Potsdam, 4 November 1989. By the beginning of November 1989 the protest movement has spread across the whole of East Germany. Everywhere, people call for freedom of the press and opinion, legalisation of opposition groups, free elections – and above all – freedom to travel.

On 8 November, West German Chancellor Kohl himself takes up the demands of the demonstrators: he tells Krenz publicly that, if the SED gives up its monopoly on power, allows independent parties and commits itself to holding free elections, he will be prepared "to talk about a completely new dimension of economic aid".

On the evening preceding 9 November, the SED leadership is forced to act; however, as Egon Krenz says the next day, "Whatever we do in this situation, we will be taking a false step."

Demonstration in East Berlin, 4 November 1989.

"The SED must renounce ist monopoly on power, must allow independent political parties and ensure free elections. Under these conditions, I am prepared to talk about a completely new dimension for our economic aid." Helmut Kohl, speech to the West German parliament, Bonn, 8 November 1989.

"Whatever we do in this situation, we're taking a false step." Egon Krenz, speech to the SED central committee, East Berlin, 9 November 1989.

9 November 1989:
Schabowski's note

Unsettled, the politburo gives the Council of Ministers the task of drawing up a travel regulation at short notice. The intention is to allow permanent departures – that is, emigration to West Germany – but only after a relevant application has been lodged. Visits – again, upon application – are to be permitted for up to thirty days a year, but are to be made contingent on the granting of a visa and the possession of a passport.

However, only around four million citizens have a passport; all others – and this is the calculation behind the plan – will at first need to apply for a passport and then wait at least a further four weeks. This is meant to prevent an immediate exodus by all citizens. The new travel regulation is not to be announced until 10 November at 4 a.m. so that the staff at the passport and registration authorities can prepare for the expected stampede. In the afternoon of 9 November, the politburo and Central Committee approve the regulation.

"Immediately, without delay!"

Egon Krenz hands the document to politburo spokesman Günter Schabowski. He gives him the task of informing the public about its content at a press conference scheduled for 6 p.m.. Schabowski was not there when the politburo approved the travel regulation at midday, nor was he in the room when Krenz read the bill to the Central Committee. For this reason, he does not know the text of the document or anything about any waiting period. At the end of his press conference, which is broadcast live by GDR state television, he reads out the travel regulation from the document that Krenz has given him. It says that GDR citizens can apply both for permanent exit and for private trips without having to fulfil the previous requirements, and that applications are to be approved quickly. It also states that permanent departures can be made via all border crossing points from the GDR to West Germany or West Berlin. "When does that go into effect?" several journalists shout. Schabowski seems at a loss, for, as he says later, "This question had never been discussed with me beforehand." He scratches his head and skims quickly through the document. He overlooks the final sentence in the resolution of the Council of Ministers, which states that the press release is not to be issued until 10 November. His eyes get caught on the words "immediately" and "without delay" at the very beginning of the document. He thus gives the brief answer: "Immediately, without delay!" A few minutes later, at 7.01 p.m., the press conference ends.

In relation to the intention behind it, Schabowski's announcement is the world's greatest disaster in the history of the press conference.

"GDR opens border"

Schabowski's announcement becomes the top story during prime news time until 8.15 p.m.. Owing to the lack of precise information, Western media begin to fill out the room for interpretation left by Schabowski, piece together what information there is and construct their own meaning. They very quickly interpret his contradictory statements as an "opening of the borders": "GDR opens borders" is already the Associated Press headline at 7.05 p.m., and at 7.41 p.m. DPA makes the "sensational announcement": "The GDR border to the Federal Republic and to West Berlin is open." The ARD news show "Tagesschau" has the new travel regulation as its top story, with the words "GDR opens border" as a background caption.

9 November 1989: International press conference

9 November 1989, 6:57 p.m.: International press conference (on the podium left-right: Central Committee members Helga Labs, Manfred Banaschak, Guenter Schabowski, Gerhard Beil).

Guenter Schabowski: […] A decision was made today, as far as I know (looking toward Helga Labs and Manfred Banaschak in hope of confirmation). A recommendation from the politburo was taken up that we take a passage from the [draft of the] travel regulation and put it into effect, that (um) — as it is called, for better or worse — that regulates permanent exit, leaving the Republic. Since we find it (um) unacceptable that this movement is taking place (um) across the territory of an allied state, (um) which is not an easy burden for that country to bear. Therefore (um), we have decided today (um) to implement a regulation that allows every citizen of the German Democratic Republic (um) to (um) leave the GDR through any of the border crossings.

Question: (many voices) When does that go into effect?…

Riccardo Ehrman, reporter, ANSA: Without a passport? Without a passport? (No, no)

Krzysztof Janowski, reporter, Voice of America: When is that in effect?… (confusion, voices…) At what point does the regulation take effect?

Guenter Schabowski: What?

Peter Brinkmann, reporter, Bild Zeitung: At once? When …?

Guenter Schabowski: (… scratches his head) You see, comrades, I was informed today (puts on his glasses as he speaks further), that such an announcement had been (um) distributed earlier today. You should actually have it already. So, (reading very quickly from the paper): "Applications for travel abroad by private individuals can now be made without the previously existing requirements (of demonstrating a need to travel or proving familial relationships). The travel authorizations will be issued within a short time. Grounds for denial will only be applied in particular exceptional cases. The responsible departments of passport and registration control in the People's Police district offices in the GDR are instructed to issue visas for permanent exit without delays and without presentation of the existing requirements for permanent exit."

Riccardo Ehrman, reporter, ANSA: With a passport?

Guenter Schabowski: (um…) (reads:) "Permanent exit is possible via all GDR border crossings to the FRG. These changes replace the temporary practice of issuing [travel] authorizations through GDR consulates and permanent exit with a GDR personal identity card via third countries." (Looks up) (um) I cannot answer the question about passports at this point. (Looks questioningly at Labs and Banaschak.) That is also a technical question. I don't know, the passports have to … so that everyone has a passport, they first have to be distributed. But we want to…

Manfred Banaschak: The substance of the announcement is decisive…

Guenter Schabowski: … is the …

Ralph T. Niemeyer, reporter, DAPA: When does it come into effect?

Guenter Schabowski: (Looks through his papers…) That comes into effect, to my knowledge, immediately, without delay (looking through his papers further).

Helga Labs: (quietly) …without delay.

Gerhard Beil: (quietly) That has to be decided by the Council of Ministers.

Krzysztof Janowski, reporter, Voice of America: In Berlin also? (…Many voices…)

Peter Brinkmann, reporter, Bild Zeitung: You only said the FRG, is the regulation also valid for West Berlin?

Guenter Schabowski: (Reading aloud quickly) "As the Press Office of the Ministry … the Council of Ministers decided that until the Volkskammer implements a corresponding law, this temporary regulation will be in effect."

Peter Brinkmann, reporter, Bild Zeitung: Does this also apply for West Berlin? You only mentioned the FRG.

Guenter Schabowski: (shrugs his shoulders, frowns, looks at his papers) So … (pause), um hmmm (reads aloud): "Permanent exit can take place via all border crossings from the GDR to the FRG and West Berlin, respectively."

Based on the account of Ralph T. Niemeyer. A confirmation by independent side is not yet available.

9/10 November 1989: Breaching the Wall

The reports in the Western media set off a rush on the border crossings and the Brandenburg Gate by East and West Berliners. And it is this rush that actually brings about the event that has already been announced – the "open border". The fall of the Wall is thus the first event in world history that took place as a result of an anticipatory announcement by press agencies, TV and radio.

On the evening of 9 November 1989, the GDR border guards, who have no information or orders from their military leaders, uneasily face growing crowds of people on both sides of the border crossings, who want to test whether the reports are true. The border guards' queries to their superiors regarding how Schabowski's remarks are to be interpreted remain unanswered, as do their superiors' queries at the next highest level, even those made to the ministries. In the evening hours, only deputies or deputies of deputies can be reached – and no one knows what to do. The communication channels to the very top. however, are closed: at first, no deputy can contact his minister, as the meeting of the Central Committee has been extended until 8.45 p.m.. For this reason, the highest echelons of the party and the government are unaware of the press conference, the media reaction it has engendered and the growing rush on the border crossings from East and West.

The rush on the Eastern side is strongest at the Bornholmer Strasse border crossing, situated in the densely populated district of Prenzlauer Berg. At first, the border guards play a waiting game and tell the people to come back the next day. They then allow some people to leave the country, but put a stamp in their identity cards to invalidate them. Without knowing it, the first East Berliners to walk over Bornholmer Bridge ("Bösebrücke") to West Berlin are deprived of their citizenship.

But in the end, the pressure in front of the barrier becomes so great that passport controllers and border soldiers begin to fear for their lives. At around 11.30 p.m. they decide on their own account to stop all border control. "We're opening the floodgates now!" the head officer tells the passport controllers; and then the barriers are opened. At Invalidenstrasse, the passport controllers are at first determined to get rid of the West and East Berliners. They call in reinforcements: 45 men with sub-machine guns. But as the situation escalates, they decide: "We are not going to shoot at unarmed people." The soldiers withdraw and the commander orders: "Let them go!"

By the early hours, all border crossings are open; a short time later, East and West Berliners celebrate the fall of the Wall under the Brandenburg Gate.

"We're opening the floodgates now! We're opening everything!"

Edwin Görlitz, lieutenant-colonel, deputy head of the Ministry for State Security passport inspection unit at the Bornholmer Strasse border crossing.

Thousands of people force the opening of the Bornholmer Strasse border crossing just around 11.30 p.m. on 9 November 1989.

Spiegel-TV reporter Georg Mascolo, cameraman Rainer März and his assistant Germar Biester crossed the processing line shortly beforehand, and so manage to document the historic moment on film.

Bornholmer Strasse crossing point, 9/10 November 1989.

Wall at the Brandenburg Gate, 9/10 November 1989: "My feelings were a mixture of joy and fear. In the end we started to hammer away at the Wall to tear it down symbolically." Conny Hanschmann (3rd left)

10 November 1989

On the morning of 10 November, Willy Brandt comes to the Brandenburg Gate. When the Wall was built, he was Mayor of Berlin. He had to watch on helplessly as concrete posts were rammed into the ground, rolls of barbed wire were laid out and families were separated. His remark, "What belongs together is now growing together" is still a political dream on this day – but one that is soon to be fulfilled.

Later in the afternoon, Brandt speaks in front of Schöneberg Town Hall alongside Mayor Walter Momper and West German Chancellor Helmut Kohl. The Chancellor has interrupted his state visit in Poland for this rally. His speech is disturbed by a barrage of whistling and booing from the supporters of the red-green Senate. Only afterwards do the dramatic events in the background become known: during the rally, Horst Teltschik, an advisor to the Chancellor, is called to the telephone in the Town Hall. The Soviet ambassador, Yuli Kvitsinski, tells him of Mikhail Gorbachev's concern that there could be violent clashes in Berlin and that Soviet facilities or even Soviet troops could be attacked. Gorbachev calls on the Chancellor not to allow the situation to get out of control.

Helmut Kohl and Horst Teltschik speculate: Is this message from Gorbachev a concerned question or a concealed threat? The Chancellor already responds in his speech in front of the Town Hall, calls for reason and calm, and rejects any form of radicalism. The next day, he reassures the Soviet Secretary-General on the telephone, telling him about the happy and peaceful mood in Berlin. Relieved at the reaction from Moscow, Horst Teltschik notes: "No threat, no warning, just the request to let prudence prevail." Moscow does not obstruct developments; the Soviet troops in the GDR – 350,000 of them – remain in their barracks.

See also: www.chronik-der-mauer.de > English > 1989 > November > 10

"What belongs together is now growing together."

Willy Brandt, 10 November 1989.

Willy Brandt at the Brandenburg Gate, 10 November 1989.

"I think that if we had gone to Berlin with combat units, there would have been a great danger of bloodshed."

A commander of the National People's Army, 1995.

Morning of 11 November 1989: attempt to tear down the Wall at Brandenburg Gate.

11 November 1989: Conflict resolution at the Brandenburg Gate

On the morning of 11 November, the Brandenburg Gate is the last centre of conflict. The anti-tank wall there has been occupied for more than 30 hours. During the night, in a mood of high spirits, people have started chiselling away at the Wall and taking down the tubing along the top; the GDR border troops bring in reinforcements. When a group of West Berliners succeeds in tearing down a segment of the Wall to the south of the Brandenburg Gate, nervousness grows.

On the Eastern side, hectic activity begins. Two elite units of the National People's Army, around 10,000 soldiers in total, have already been put on increased alert the day before; the situation now threatens to escalate. Defence Minister Kessler obviously fears that there will be a rush on the Brandenburg Gate. At around 10.15 a.m., he rings up the commander of the land forces, Colonel General Horst Stechbarth. Stechbarth hears his minister ask him whether he is prepared to march to Berlin with two regiments to clear the Wall at the Brandenburg Gate. Stechbarth asks the minister to reassess the situation and consider whether other means can be used, pointing out that the consequences of moving troops to Berlin in the present situation cannot be foreseen.

And the security forces in West and East Berlin do in fact find other means: border soldiers manage to clear the Wall peacefully and occupy it themselves; West Berlin police block off the access routes to the area near the Wall with police vans. The piece of Wall that has been removed is lifted back and welded on again. It is the last time that a part of the Wall is repaired in Berlin. By midday, the situation is calmer; the alert status of the National People's Army units is lifted. "I think that if we had gone to Berlin with combat units," says one of the commanders afterwards, "there would have been a great danger of bloodshed."

German President Richard von Weizsäcker at Potsdamer Platz, 12 November 1989.

12 November 1989: Potsdamer Platz

Richard von Weizsäcker, former German President "Schabowski did not actually announce that the Wall was open. In fact, the media spread their own interpretation of the announcement, which went further than what the GDR's leaders had decided. And then came the first successful crossing of the border at Bornholmer Strasse in the night of 9 November, because the border guards didn't know how to react. On 12 November 1989, I took a walk on my own to Potsdamer Platz amid the general feeling that no one really knew what was right and what was allowed – particularly the border soldiers. Strictly speaking, the German president can't really just walk around as he likes and take on the role of a reconnaissance patrol in an uncertain political situation. But I just wanted to go out.

Opening of a new border crossing point on Potsdamer Platz, 500 metres south of the Brandenburg Gate, 12 November 1989.

"Mr. President, no unusual occurrences to report."

So I walked from the western side of Potsdamer Platz over the broad, empty space towards the east. I saw how I was being watched by the border guards through binoculars. Then a senior officer came towards me with meticulous military demeanour and said: 'Mr. President, no unusual occurrences to report.' I felt that probably no other words could have been in starker contrast to the remarkable events of this time."

"We are one people!"

The breach of the Wall on 9 November 1989 means more than just an "opening of the border": it is an act of self-liberation. The power of the event, its form and symbolism, tears the control of the border – and thus also the control over the no longer imprisoned people of the GDR – out of the hands of the SED. Without the Wall, the SED leadership also sees itself deprived of its most important lever in negotiations with the West German government on economic stabilisation; the regime has lost the last creditworthy property of the GDR.

At the same time, the pressure on the party and the state continues to grow after the fall of the Wall. On the one hand, emigration to West Germany increases again by leaps and bounds: from 10 November to the end of 1989, over 120,000 people leave the GDR (total figure for 1989: 343,854); 180,000 more leave from January to March 1990. On the other hand, however, mass demonstrations continue even in the second half of November. The crowds soon change their chant from "We are the people" to "We are one people"; banners with the words "Germany – United Father-land" and black, red and gold flags without the GDR emblem soon predominate at demonstrations everywhere in the GDR.

At round-table conferences, the new democratic movements and parties restrict the power of the SED, make it give up its monopoly on leader-ship as enshrined in the GDR constitution and force it to agree to free elections. Within a few weeks, the central party structures fall apart; polit-buro, Central Committee Secretariat and Central Committee all disband. Without the control centre of the party, the state power structures crumble; almost unnoticed, the National Defence Council simply ceases to exist for lack of members. Citizens' committees occupy the district State Security buildings and prevent files from being destroyed.

The demonstrators change their chant from "We are the people" to "We are one people".

Deconstruction of the US control building at Checkpoint Charlie in the presence of the foreign ministers of the four Allied states, the GDR and West Germany, 22 June 1990.

After the fall of the Wall and the end of the old SED, the Soviet Union is the last guarantor for the existence of the GDR as a state. At first, the Soviet leaders vigorously oppose any tendencies towards uniting the two German states. But in January 1990, the Soviet Union's own domestic problems – increasing ethnic conflicts, the serious economic and supply crisis, its looming inability to repay its debts to the West and the disintegration of the Warsaw Pact – and the inexorable decline of the SED's power quickly make it apparent that the GDR cannot be maintained. Mikhail Gorbachev gives the green light for German unification.

"German reunification was ultimately a process as inavoidable as it was legitimate. [...] Presumably some time will pass before a German nation that has undergone many changes has overcome the wounds of the past."

Mikhail Gorbachev, Memoirs, New York 1996.

The first free parliamentary election on 18 March 1990, from which the CDU-led "Alliance for Germany" (Allianz für Deutschland) emerges as strongest party with 48.1 percent of votes, becomes a clear vote in favour of taking the fast track to German unity.

On 21 June 1990, the GDR parliament and the West German Bundestag approve a treaty on economic, monetary and social union with two-thirds majorities. This results in the DM being introduced in the GDR as the official currency on 1 July 1990.

The negotiations on the external aspects of unity are carried out at "two-plus-four conferences" attended by both Germanies and the four Second World War Allies, as well as in numerous bilateral talks. They are concluded on 12 September with the signing of the "Treaty on the Final Settlement with Respect to Germany". In this treaty, the occupying powers give up the rights and responsibilities they took on in connection with the Second World War in Berlin and Germany as a whole. Germany is give sovereign rights over its internal and external affairs, confirms the final character of its borders and commits itself to not carry out any wars of aggression and to reducing the Bundeswehr to 370,000 personnel. The withdrawal of the 350,000 soldiers of the Western Group of the Soviet armed forces from the GDR by 1994 is also agreed upon.

In the "Treaty on the Final Settlement with Respect to Germany" the four Second World War Allies, Great Britain, USA, France and the Soviet Union, give up the rights and responsibilities they took on in Berlin and Germany as a whole. Germany is given sovereign rights over its internal and external affairs.

On 3 October 1990, the process of unification is officially concluded.

On the domestic front, the most important steps on the path to unification are the GDR's resolution of 23 August to join the Federal Republic according to Article 23 of the constitution, and the unification treaty between the two German states that creates the legal foundation for the two countries to unite as one.

Both parliaments approve this treaty on 20 September 1990, thus also approving the goal of creating equal living conditions in Germany after forty years of separation. On 3 October 1990, the process of unification is officially concluded.

Celebrating German Unity at the Brandenburg Gate in Berlin, 3 October 1990.

Reflections

George Bush, President of the United States "On the 10th of November, Gorbachev sent me a telegram of considerable anxiety. I found it understandable that he was worried and now wanted to tell me about the problems that this event was causing to him. We knew that the pressures on Gorbachev were enormous. Inside the Warsaw Pact and the Soviet hegemonic empire East Germany was the jewel of the crown.

We did not know how far this monumental event would affect the pride of the Soviet military, the nationalist feeling that the Soviet empire had. And here it was crumbling, right in front of their eyes. How would they react? Nobody knew for sure. So what do you do? You act prudently. You support the Germans, you say, this is wonderful, but you don`t do it in a way not to cause problems that you can't foresee.

Later I had some differences with Margaret Thatcher and François Mitterrand, because I was much more forwardleaning on the side of Chancellor Kohl on German unification. But at the time of these criticals days in November both of them shared my view that we should not overreact and cause problems for Gorbachev that might get out of control, in other words: that might cause his more reactionary elements to kick him out, to start rattling the saber and have Germany and Berlin back in some kind of a military confrontation."

Meeting of
Mikhail Gorbachev (center),
George Bush (right) and
Helmut Kohl (left)
in Germany,
November 1999.

Mikhail Gorbachev, CPSU General Secretary "Everyone – Bush, Mitterrand and Thatcher – recognised the seriousness of the situation. Possibly, someone even thought of somehow slowing down this process. Like the others, I followed the developments very closely, with a sense of responsibility and with caution. We were all cautious. But I think that our caution was justified in this case. And at the same time everyone took a different position; let's put it like that. And this is all the more important in view of the fact that in the end we reached a common position. And we reached a united position because everyone, despite all differences of opinion, nonetheless had sympathy at this moment: sympathy for the longing of the Germans to live in one land, to unite. In my opinion, that was very important and shows how serious the politicians involved in this process were.

9 November 1989, the German unification process, is one of the most important phases in German history, in our history, in European history, in world history. And in history, one phase follows another. For this reason, we must all think of the future. And the future demands of us that we act responsibly and preserve the trust invested in us."

Helmut Kohl, West German Chancellor "We had to act fast. And that was the reason why it was so important to find the necessary support. There is no doubt that my personal relationship of trust above all to George Bush, François Mitterrand and, in the end, to Mikhail Gorbachev played an important role in this situation. In this regard, we had a fortunate configuration – which did not just come about on its own, however, but which we had done something towards.

There is no question: without George Bush and without Mikhail Gorbachev – they were the two decisive personalities – German unification would not have happened. Of course, what we ourselves did in Germany – in particular the protests, the mass gatherings of our compatriots in Leipzig and other places – had a very great significance. But if the two superpowers had not moved with us towards German unification, things would have been very different. That is my lasting conviction."

The legal prosecution of the fatal shootings at the Berlin Wall

In the years after 1990, the Berlin State Prosecutor brings 112 charges against 246 people in connection with the acts of violence at the Berlin Wall: against "Wall snipers" and their military and political superiors. All trials have been concluded.

More than half of the accused are acquitted: in many cases, the person who fired the fatal shot(s) can no longer be established; in others, no intent to kill can be proven. Shots fired at armed military deserters are even legitimated by a decision of the supreme court: the Federal High Court rules that desertion is a crime according to the GDR military penal law of 1962. The killing of deserters, it says, is excused because, in this "special case", the unlawfulness of the deed could not be apparent to those who carried out the shootings.

A total of 132 of the accused have final sentences passed on them for various manslaughter offences – as direct or indirect offenders, as accessories, instigators or for aiding and abetting – including
- 10 members of the SED leadership
- 42 members of the military leadership and
- 80 border soldiers.

As well as the cases in Berlin, the Neuruppin State Prosecutor brings 21 charges against 39 border soldiers who fired fatal shots and 12 commanding officers; in these 31 cases, the shots were fired on the Outer Ring around West Berlin.

19 of the accused soldiers are given suspended sentences for manslaughter, and one border soldier is convicted to ten years' imprisonment for the murder of Walter Kittel. 17 of the accused are found not guilty; the cases against two soldiers cannot be opened for health reasons. All 12 commanding officers are given suspended sentences.

"For the protection of the workers' and farmers' power": The SED leadership celebrating the 40th anniversary of the GDR border troops, East Berlin 1986.

"Firearms are to be ruthlessly used in the event of attempts to break through the border, and the comrades who have successfully used their firearms are to be commended."

Erich Honecker, 1974.

When establishing the guilt of a person and handing down punishments, the courts take subjective extenuating factors in favour of the accused into great account, such as
- their integration into the hierarchy of a totalitarian system,
- the repression of justified doubts regarding state-given orders
- the constant political indoctrination with the resultant deformation of the sense of what is right
- the time that has passed since the crime
- the young age of the accused at the time of the crime and
- the advanced age of the accused at the time of sentencing, with the resultant increase in sensitivity to punishment.

The prison sentences are graded according to the position of the accused in the military and political hierarchy, and on the whole are surprisingly short.

The border troops as part of the (secret) police and military dictatorship

Border guards	6–24 months (usually suspended)
Regiment commanders	20–30 months
Commanders-in-chief (and their deputies) of a border brigade or Centre Border Command	6–39 months
Commander-in-chief of the border troops (and his deputies) and members of the NVA leadership	2–78 months
Members of the SED leadership	36–78 months
Members of the National Defence Council	60–90 months

Following the preliminary examination and after it has been established that the killing of a person was also a punishable offence in the GDR, the German federal courts apply West German law when giving verdicts and fixing sentences. This law is – with a few exceptions – more favourable to the accused than GDR law, because it is more lenient. The courts' verdicts follow the jurisdiction of the Federal High Court, according to which the deliberate killing of unarmed escapees cannot be justified, as it is "an obvious, unbearable offence against fundamental dictates of justice and against human rights that are protected under international law." Orders, regulations and laws that allowed the use of firearms to prevent escapes and thus, ultimately, to kill escapees, are therefore not recognised as sufficient justification.

Bullet lodged in the heart: the Stasi archived the Kalashnikov bullet that killed Christian Buttkus on 4 March 1965. 21-year-old Buttkus attempted to escape to West Berlin from Kleinmachnow with his fiancée.

In view of the way an entire people was imprisoned and the killing, wounding, criminalisation of and discrimination against a large number of people, many find the number of acquittals too high and the punishments that are given too lenient. The suffering of many families and the injustice done to several generations in the GDR remain largely unatoned for.

However, we do owe it to the criminal justice system that, because of the investigations and trials, the human rights violations in the GDR and the crimes committed by the SED have been comprehensively documented.

The demolition of the Wall

At the same time as preparations for German unification are going ahead, the Wall in Berlin disappears. Its dismantling starts with the opening of new border crossings. Countless "Wallpeckers" hammer and chisel away at the concrete barrier and remove their own personal souvenir. The border soldiers look on helplessly. Since 14 November 1989, the "order to shoot" has been officially revoked: order at the Wall disintegrates and guarding it becomes increasingly pointless. Military leaders complain that soldiers are selling parts of their uniform while on duty and that officers are accepting presents and getting drunk.

At the end of December, the first dog runs, spotlights and signal fences are taken down. In February, the Wall is pulled down at Potsdamer Platz and in June in Bernauer Strasse. The 1.90-metre-high mesh fence that replaces it in some parts already loses its function on 1 July 1990: on this day, all controls on persons between the two German states cease. On 30 September 1990, the GDR border troops are disbanded and all guns and pistols are collected – 54,260 firearms and 3,060 tonnes of ammunition. For their last mission, the border soldiers, who from 3 October 1990 are integrated into the West German Bundeswehr as a "Disbandment and Recultivation Detachment", need no weapons.

Using 65 cranes, 175 trucks and 13 bulldozers, they almost completely remove the barrier system in the inner-city area by the end of 1990. The demolition work finishes at the end of 1992 at the Outer Ring, which now forms the border between the states of Berlin and Brandenburg.

In Berlin, not even a small segment of the death strip, with its walls, signal fences, barriers and watchtowers, can be preserved to commemorate the deadly border regime. The hatred of this construction is too great – and the interest in capitalising on the real estate in the best area of Berlin awakens too quickly. Only in Bernauer Strasse, Niederkirchner Strasse and Mühlenstrasse ("East Side Gallery") do some fairly long segments of the Wall remain standing.

"Wallpeckers" chipping away at the concrete.

Wall destroyed by "wallpeckers" in Berlin-Mitte, 1990.

Storage for demolished wall elements, September 1990.

Some of the segments of the Wall that have been painted on are auctioned in Berlin and Monte Carlo as "contemporary art objects" and "keystones in the longest art work of the world", while others are given away to institutions in Germany and abroad as memorials to the end of the Cold War. The GDR Council of Ministers even makes over eight segments of the Wall to the American sculptor Edwina Sandys, a granddaughter of Winston Churchill, to commemorate the famous speech by her grandfather in Fulton, USA.

More than 40,000 segments of the Wall are crushed for use as granules in road building. Some segments are still to be found in cement works where they now separate different sorts of gravel from one another – instead of people.

The Berlin Wall in Tonnes (1990–1992)

Cement	180,000 tonnes
Asbestos	15,000 tonnes
Scrap	6,000 tonnes
Plastics	3,000 tonnes
Wood, insulation materials, etc.	100 tonnes

East Side Gallery

In spring 1990, numerous German and foreign artists paint the Wall in the district of Friedrichshain. The section of border between Schilling Bridge and Oberbaum Bridge selected for this art happening is where several people have died while trying to escape. Most of the paintings have to do with freedom and human rights. A preservation order is put on the "East Side Gallery" in 1991 as an art site. At 1.3 kilometres, it is the longest section of the Berlin Wall to be preserved.

See also: www.chronik-der-mauer.de/remnants > Station 14

"My God, help me to survive this deadly love."

Service

Information for visitors to Berlin

Berlin Tourismus & Kongress GmbH
Am Karlsbad 11, 10785 Berlin
Tel.: +49 (0) 30 - 25 00 2333
info@visitberlin.de
www.visitberlin.de

Information for visitors to Potsdam

Potsdam Marketing and Service GmbH –
Tourist Information Centre
Luisenplatz 3, 14471 Potsdam
Tel.: +49 (0) 331 – 27 55 88 99
info@potsdamtourismus.de
www.potsdamtourismus.de

Museums and Memorial Sites

Allied Museum

The Allied Museum presents a permanent collection and special exhibitions documenting the presence of the Western victorious powers of the Second World War and the Cold War in Berlin.

The museum contains numerous exhibits, ranging from items connected with the "Berlin Air Lift" in 1948 / 49 to the world-famous sentry box at Checkpoint Charlie. It also provides detailed information on events spanning nearly five decades – up to the time when the Western Allies pulled out of Berlin in 1990.

Alliierten Museum
Clayallee 135, 14195 Berlin-Zehlendorf

Tel.: +49 (0) 30 - 81 81 99 0
info@AlliiertenMuseum.de
www.alliiertenmuseum.de

Open daily except Mondays
10 a.m. – 6 p.m.

Admission free

Guided tours in German, English and French by appointment

S-Bahn: S 1 to "Zehlendorf", then Bus No. 115 (direction U-Güntzelstrasse) to "Alliierten Museum"
U-Bahn: U 3 to "Oskar-Helene-Heim"
Bus: Nos. 115, X 83 to "AlliiertenMuseum"

German-Russian Museum Berlin-Karlshorst

This museum chronicles the history of the Second World War – particularly in the East, where the conflict was at its bloodiest – and post-war history up to 1991.

On May 8, the unconditional surrender of the German Wehrmacht was signed in the museum's large hall, a former officers' mess, putting an end to Nazi rule in Germany and Europe. Subsequently, the building housed the headquarters of the Soviet Military Administration in Germany.

The museum is a place for many different kinds of encounter between Germans and Russians, and presents in-depth information on the history of German-Russian relations in the 20th century.

Deutsch-Russisches Museum Berlin-Karlshorst
Zwieseler Strasse 4 (corner of Rheinstein-strasse), 10318 Berlin

Tel.: +49 (0) 30 - 50 15 08 10
kontakt@museum-karlshorst.de
www.museum-karlshorst.de

S-Bahn: S 3 to "Bahnhof Karlshorst"
(exit Treskowallee), then Bus No. 296

Open from Tuesday to Sunday
10 a.m. – 6 p.m.

Admission free

Guided group tours by appointment

Berlin Wall Memorial

The Berlin Wall Memorial is the central memorial site of German division. Its exterior site contains the last piece of the Berlin Wall with the preserved grounds behind it, giving an impression of the structure of the East German border system up to the end of the 1980s.
In addition, a permanent exhibition opened in 2014 shows the political backdrop to the building of the Wall in 1961 all the way to its fall in 1989. The memorial is part of the Berlin Wall Foundation, which also includes the Marienfelde Refugee Center Museum.

Gedenkstätte Berliner Mauer
Bernauer Str. 111/119, 13355 Berlin
Tel.: +49 (0) 30 – 467 98 66 66
besucherservice@stiftung-berliner-mauer.de
www.berliner-mauer-gedenkstaette.de

Open daily except Mondays
10 a.m. – 6 p.m.
The open-air-exhibition on the former border strip is open 24-7

Admission free

Guided tours in German, English, French, Italian and Spanish by appointment
S-Bahn: S 1 or S 2 to "Nordbahnhof"
U-Bahn: U 8 to "Bernauer Strasse"
Tram: M 10 to "Gedenkstätte Berliner Mauer"

Chapel of Reconciliation

The Chapel of Reconciliation, a part of the Berlin Wall Memorial, is a site of commemoration as well as a place of worship and prayer. When the Wall was put up in 1961, this Protestant church ended up in the "death strip", inaccessible to its congregation. In 1985 the East German government ordered it to be blown up.

On November 9 1999, ten years after the Wall came down, the topping-out ceremony of the Chapel was celebrated on the foundations of the Reconciliation Church, and the building was consecrated exactly one year later.

A prayer service, open to the public, is held Tuesdays to Fridays from 12 midday to 12.15 p.m. to remember a person who died at the Berlin Wall.

Kapelle der Versöhnung
Bernauer Strasse 4, 10115 Berlin

Tel.: +49 (0) 30 - 463 60 34
info@kapelle-versoehnung.de
www.kapelle-versoehnung.de

Open from Tuesday to Sunday
10 a.m. – 5 p.m.
Service of Worship: Sunday 10 a.m.
Devotion and prayer Friday 4 p.m.
(Coventry Service) and Saturday 12 midday
Admission free

S-Bahn: S 1, S 2 or S 25 to "Nordbahnhof",
then Bus No. 245 to "Bernauer Strasse"
U-Bahn: U 8 to "Bernauer Strasse"
Tram: M 10 to "Gedenkstätte Berliner Mauer"

Marienfelde Refugee Center Museum

In the former Marienfelde Refugee Center,
the history of East German refugees from
1949 to 1990 is commemorated.
It documents the reasons why people
fled the GDR and the routes they took,
the procedures they went through to be
admitted to West Germany and what
happened to them afterwards. The
museum is part of the Berlin Wall
Foundation, which also includes the
Berlin Wall Memorial.

Erinnerungsstätte Notaufnahmelager
Marienfelde
Marienfelder Allee 66–80, 12277 Berlin

Tel.: +49 (0) 30 - 75 00 84 00
info-enm@stiftung-berliner-mauer.de
www.notaufnahmelager-berlin.de

Open from Tuesday to Sunday
10 a.m. – 6 p.m.

Admission free

Guided tours
Wednesday and Sunday 3 p.m.

Fee: € 2.50, concession € 1.50

Group tours by appointment

S-Bahn: S 2 to "Marienfelde"
Bus: M 77 to "Stegerwaldstrasse"

Berlin-Hohenschönhausen Memorial

This memorial commemorates the 44-year
history of political persecution in the Soviet
occupation zone and the GDR. The Soviet
occupying power first built a "special camp"
here. After it was closed in October 1946,
the main Soviet remand prison for Germany
was housed in the basement of the building.
In 1952 the GDR'S Ministry for State Security
took over the prison, using it as its main
detention centre until 1989.

Gedenkstätte Berlin-Hohenschönhausen
Genslerstrasse 66, 13055 Berlin

Tel.: +49 (0) 30 - 98 60 82 30
info@stiftung-hsh.de
www.stiftung-hsh.de

The former prison can be visited only on
guided tours.

Guided tours for individual visitors in English:
April to October: daily at 11.30 a.m. and
2.30 p.m.
November to March: Monday to Friday at
2.30 p.m. at weekends 11.30 a.m. and
2.30 p.m.

Group tours daily from 9 a.m. to
4 p.m. by advance booking:
Tel.: +49 (0) 30 - 98 60 82 30
Fax: +49 (0) 30 - 98 60 82 34

Admission: € 6, concession € 3,
school pupils € 1

Tram: M 5 to "Freienwalder Strasse"
M 6 to "Genslerstrasse / Freienwalder
Strasse"

Stasi-Museum/Normannenstrasse Research and Memorial Center

The former headquarters of the Ministry for State Security (Stasi) now houses a Stasi-Museum focused on East Germany's political system. The permanent exhibition "State Security in the SED Dictatorship" illustrates and explains the structure, development and operations of the Stasi. The Stasi-Museum is run by members of the organisation Anti-Stalinist Action Berlin-Normannenstrasse (ASTAK), founded in 1990. The permanent exhibition was developed by the ASTAK association in cooperation with the Agency of the Federal Commissioner for Stasi-Records (BStU).

Stasi-Museum/ASTAK e.V.
Ruschestraße 103/Haus 1, 10365 Berlin

Tel.: +49 (0)30 - 553 68 54
info@stasimuseum.de
www.stasimuseum.de

Open: Monday to Friday 10 a.m. – 6 p.m.
Weekend and Holidays 11 a.m. – 6 p.m.

Admission: € 6 (adults), € 4,50 (reduced: students, traines, senior citizens), € 3 (schoolchildren 12 years and older) Concessions for groups of more than 10 people

Guided tours are available in German, English, French, Italian and Danish and need to be booked in advance

U-Bahn: U 5 to "Magdalenenstrasse", Ruschestrasse exit

Police Historical Collection of the Berlin Police President

In addition to a range of different special exhibitions, the Berlin Police Headquarters presents a permanent collection documenting eight decades of police history in Berlin. The exhibition covers many facets of police activity, from everyday policing in the past and present, to a display of uniforms, weapons and implements used in various criminal cases. Among the museum's exhibits is the sentry box used by the West Berlin Customs Office at Glienicke Bridge.

Polizeihistorische Sammlung des Polizeipräsidenten in Berlin
Platz der Luftbrücke 6, 12101 Berlin

Tel.: +49 (0) 30 - 46 64 99 47 62
phs@polizei.berlin.de
www.berlin.de / polizei /verschiedenes/
polizei-historische-sammlung.de

Open from Monday to Wednesday
9 a.m. – 3 p.m.

Guided tours Monday to Friday
by appointment

Admission: € 2, concession € 1,
guided tours € 25 plus € 1 per person

U-Bahn: U 6 to "Platz der Luftbrücke"
Bus: Nos. 104, 248 "U-Bahnhof
Platz der Luftbrücke" / Columbiadamm

Berlin Wall Museum

The privately financed museum, situated at the former Allied sector crossing point, documents the history of the Berlin Wall in German, English, French and Russian. The museum "Haus am Checkpoint Charlie", opened on 14 June 1963 by Rainer Hildebrandt, has several themed exhibition areas, including "The Wall – history and occurrences", "Original artefacts from successful escapes under, on and over the ground" and "It happened at Checkpoint Charlie".

Museum "Haus am Checkpoint Charlie"
Friedrichstrasse 43-45, 10969 Berlin

Tel.: +49 (0) 30 - 2 53 72 50
info@mauermuseum.de
www.mauermuseum.de

Open daily 9 a.m. – 10 p.m.

Admission: Adults € 12,50,
school pupils and students € 9,50,
groups of over 20 people € 8,50

U-Bahn: U6 to "Kochstrasse",
U2 to "Stadtmitte"
Bus: M 29

Lindenstrasse Memorial Site, Potsdam

Located in the heart of historic Potsdam, the Lindenstrasse memorial site is a unique place of memory. With its history under National Socialism as well as in the Soviet Occupation Zone and GDR, it is a symbol of the political persecution and violence practiced during two different German dictatorships in the course of the twentieth century. At the same time it stands for the efforts to overcome communist one-party rule, and

the victory of democracy ushered in by the Peaceful Revolution of 1989-90.
After the building was taken over by the GDR secret police in 1952, it was used as a remand prison for political prisoners until 1989. Nearly 7,000 men and women were subject here to inhumane conditions of detention and brutal interrogation techniques by the Stasi up until 1989.

Gedenkstätte Lindenstrasse
Lindenstrasse 54, 14467 Potsdam

Tel.: +49 (0) 331 - 289 6136
Fax: +49 (0) 331 - 289 6137
info@gedenkstaette-lindenstrasse.de
www.gedenkstaette-lindenstrasse.de
Open Tuesday to Sunday, 10 a.m. – 6 p.m.

Admission: € 1,50; with guided tour: € 3
€ 1 for pupils, with guided tour: € 2

Tram 91 (Pirschheide), Tram 94 (Pirschheide), Bus 605 (Golm-Bahnhof), Bus 606 (Alt-Golm) to "Dortustrasse", 5 min. walk to the memorial site

Villa Schöningen, Potsdam

Villa Schöningen is a Cold War Museum which is located adjacent to the Glienicke Bridge in Potsdam. Built from 1843 – 45 by Ludwig Persius, architect to the King of Prussia, Villa Schöningen houses a historical exhibition on the story of the Glienicke Bridge during the Cold War ("Spies. Wall. Children's home – at the bridge between the worlds"). Computer screens serve as the principal medium to communicate texts, photos and videos.

In addition Villa Schöningen hosts temporary exhibitions of contemporary art.

Villa Schöningen
Berliner Strasse 86, 14467 Potsdam

T +49 (0) 331-200 17 41
presse@villa-schoeningen.de
www.villa-schoeningen.de

Open from Thursday to Sunday
10 a.m. – 6 p.m.

Admission: € 9, concession € 7

Tram: From Potsdam main station:
93 to "Glienicker Brücke"
S-Bahn: From Berlin: S 1 or S 7
to Wannsee Bhf;
Bus No. 316 to "Glienicker Brücke"

German Historical Museum

This museum, housed in the historic "Zeug-haus" (Arsenal) on Unter den Linden, looks back over 2,000 years of German history. Its 7,500 square metres of exhibition space contain 8,000 selected exhibits and multi-media presentations that provide a vivid picture of the past.
On the first floor, the comprehensive display takes visitors from the first century to the end of the empire in 1918, while on the ground floor it ranges from the history of the Weimar Republic, the Nazi regime, the post-war era and the two German states to the withdrawal of the World War II Allies in 1994. The museum's permanent collection is supplemented by changing special exhibitions that often focus on contemporary history.

Deutsches Historisches Museum
Unter den Linden 2, 10117 Berlin

Info-phone: +49 (0) 30 - 203 04 -444
Bookings for group visits:
+49 (0) 30 - 20 30 47 50
or +49 (0) 30 - 20 30 47 51
www.dhm.de

Open daily 10 a.m. – 6 p.m.

Admission: € 8, under 18 years of age: free

S-Bahn: S 5, S 7, S 75, S 9
to "Hackescher Markt";
S 1, S 2, S 25, S 5, S 7, S 75, S 9
to "Friedrichstrasse"
U-Bahn: U 6 to "Französische Strasse" or
"Friedrichstrasse"; U 2 to "Hausvogteiplatz"

The Story of Berlin

This privately-run exhibition takes visitors on a journey through 800 years of Berlin history: from the first mention as a trading centre in the 13th century to the present day.
The history of Berlin can be heard, seen, smelt and felt in walk-through displays featuring light-and-sound shows, slide and video projections and touchscreens.

The Story of Berlin
Kurfürstendamm 207 – 208, 10719 Berlin
(in the "Ku'Damm Karree")

Tel.: +49 (0) 30 - 88 72 01 00
info@story-of-berlin.de
www.story-of-berlin.de

Open daily 10 a.m. – 8 p.m.
(last entry 6 p.m.)

Admission: € 12, concession € 9.
groups of 8 or more € 9,
school groups per person € 5,

hildren from 6 to 14 € 5, family ticket
(2 adults and up to 3 children) € 25

S-Bahn: S 3, S 5, S 7, S 8, S 9, S 75 to
"Savignyplatz" oder "Zoologischer Garten"
U-Bahn: U 15 to "Uhlandstrasse", U 9 to
"Kurfürstendamm", U 2 to "Zoologischer
Garten"
Bus: Nos. X10, 109, 110, 119, 129, 219
to "Uhlandstrasse", No. 249 to "Lietzen-
burger Strasse / Uhlandstrasse"

GDR Museum Berlin

This privately financed museum looks back
at everyday life in the former East Germany.
It is one of the most interactive museums of
the world. The collection, divided into different
themed sections, presents everyday objects
that can be touched and handled: visitors can
take the driver's seat in a "Trabi", experience
a simulated ride through an East German
prefab housing estate and rummage in a
Carat wall unit of the kind typically found in
living rooms in the former GDR.

DDR Museum Berlin
Karl-Liebknecht-Strasse 1, 10178 Berlin
(right near the Spree River, opposite the
Berlin Cathedral)

Tel.: +49 (0) 30 - 847 12 37 31 (ticket office),
+49 (0) 30 - 847 12 37 30 (administration)
post@ddr-museum.de
www.ddr-museum.de

Open daily 10 a.m. – 8 p.m.,
Saturday till 10 p.m.

Admission: € 7, concession € 5,
€ 5 per person for groups

"Palace of Tears" at Friedrichstrasse Station

Leave-taking and longing, resentment and
despair. The emotional experience of leaving
East Germany for West Germany is never
as intense as at Berlin's Friedrichstrasse
Station border crossing point, called the
Tränenpalast, "Palace of Tears". Here,
people directly experience the impact of a
divided Germany on their personal lives.
The Foundation Haus der Geschichte der
Bundesrepublik Deutschland presents
the "Border Experiences – Everyday life in
Divided Germany" permanent exhibition
at the original location of the Tränenpalast,
now a listed building. With a combination
of real-life stories, original objects and
interviews with contemporary witnesses, the
exhibition provides a vivid insight into life in
the shadow of division and the border. The
display also presents the key turning points
in the reunification process.

Tränenpalast am Bahnhof Friedrichstrasse,
Reichstagufer 17, 10117 Berlin

Tel: +49 (0) 30 - 46 77 77 9 11
berlin@hdg.de
www.hdg.de/berlin/traenenpalast

Open: Tuesday to Friday from 9 a.m. – 7 p.m.,
Saturday, Sunday and public holidays from
10 a.m. – 6 p.m.

Admission free

S-Bahn: S 1, S 2, S 25, S 3, S 5, S 7, S 75
to "Friedrichstrasse Station"
U-Bahn: U 6 to "Friedrichstrasse Station"
U 2 to "Stadtmitte Station"
Tram: 12, M 1 to "Friedrichstrasse Station"

Museum in the Kulturbrauerei

"Everyday life in the GDR" is the subject of the permanent exhibition presented by the Foundation Haus der Geschichte der Bundesrepublik Deutschland in the Kulturbrauerei. It shows the complex tension between the expectations of the political system and the real living conditions of the people in the GDR.

Museum in der Kulturbrauerei
Knaackstraße 97, Gebäude 6.2,
10435 Berlin

Tel: +49 (0) 30 - 46 77 77 9 11
berlin@hdg.de
www.hdg.de/berlin/
museum-in-der-kulturbrauerei

Open: Tuesday to Friday from 9 a.m. – 7 p.m.,
Saturday, Sunday and public holidays from
10 a.m. - 6 p.m.

Admission free

U-Bahn: U 2 to "Eberswalder Strasse"
Station
Tram: M 1, M 10 and Tram 12 to
"Eberswalder Strasse" Station

Further Memorial Sites

The Watchtower at Kieler Eck – Memorial for Guenter Litfin

This memorial and documentation centre commemorates Guenter Litfin, the first person to be shot dead at the Berlin Wall. It presents original documents and multimedia information, as well as providing seminar facilities.

Gedenkstätte Günther Litfin e.V.
Kieler Straße 2, 10115 Berlin
Tel.: +49 (0)30 23 62 61 83;
+49 (0)163 379 72 90
info@gedenkstaetteguenterlitfin.de
www.gedenkstaetteguenterlitfin.de

Open from March to October
Sunday to Thursday, 11.30 a.m. – 14.00 p.m.

Admission free

U-Bahn: U 6 to "Schwartzkopffstrasse"
Bus: No. 120 from "Bahnhof Friedrichstrasse" to "Bundeswehrkrankenhaus"

Checkpoint Bravo – Memorial site and meeting place – Dreilinden / Drewitz border control point

"Checkpoint Bravo" was the name given by the Western allies to the Dreilinden border control point on the West Berlin side. Of the GDR Drewitz border crossing point on the other side, only the watchtower of the border troops command is still preserved.

The watchtower serves as a political education venue as well as a meeting place. A permanent exhibition provides information on the history of the site.

Checkpoint Bravo – Erinnerungs- und
Begegnungstätte – Grenzkontrollpunkt
Dreilinden / Drewitz
Albert-Einstein-Ring 45,
14532 Kleinmachnow

www.checkpoint-bravo.de

Open from June to October
Sunday 10 a.m. – 6 p.m.w

Admission free

Group guided tours by appointment
+49 (0) 332 03 - 2 48 70

How to get there by car: A 115 motorway,
exit Kleinmachnow Europarc

Bergfelde Watchtower – Nature Conservation Tower of the Deutsche Waldjugend

This former border watchtower between the
Berlin district of Frohnau and the district of
Bergfelde in Hohen Neuendorf has been a
nature conservation centre of the Deutsche
Waldjugend since 1990. It offers a wide range
of activities, especially for young people.

Deutsche Waldjugend / Naturschutzturm
Berliner Nordrand e.V.
16535 Hohen Neuendorf

Marian Przybilla:
Tel.: +49 (0) 33 03 - 50 98 44,
+49 (0)171 - 543 78 43

kontakt@naturschutzturm.de
www.naturschutzturm.de

Open on Friday 3 p.m. – 5 p.m.
and by appointment
S-Bahn: S 1 to "Hohen Neuendorf" S-Bahn
station, then by foot along Bahnstrasse,
Hainweg, Parkstrasse and the forest path
that joins onto it
Bus: No. 125 from Berlin-Frohnau S-Bahn
station to "Hubertusweg", then by foot along
Klarastrasse

Nieder Neuendorf Watchtower

In this well-preserved former command
centre of the border troops, an exhibition
provides information about German division,
daily life at the border, the East German
border security devices and various escape
attempts.

Wachturm Nieder Neuendorf
Dorfstrasse, 16761 Nieder Neuendorf

For more information:
Stadtinformation Hennigsdorf,
Rathausplatz 1, 16761 Hennigsdorf

Tel.: +49 (0) 3302 - 877 320
stadtinformation@hennigsdorf.de
www.hennigsdorf.de

Open from April to October, 10 a.m. – 18 p.m.

Admission free

Bus: 136 (Hennigsdorf – Spandau) to Nieder
Neuendorf, "Am Oberjaegerweg"

Schlesischer Busch Watchtower

The Schlesischer Busch command post on
Puschkinallee is one of two towers of this
kind that were preserved in Berlin.
The neighbouring Flutgraben e.V. association shows a permanent exhibition here on
the history of the site, as well as changing
art exhibitions.

Wachturm Schlesischer Busch
Flutgraben e.V.
Am Flutgraben 3, 12435 Berlin

Tel.: +49 (0) 30 - 53 21 96 58
www.flutgraben.org/locations/grenzwachturm/

Open: May to October
Saturday 11 a.m. – 2 p.m.
Sunday 11 a.m. – 5 p.m. and by appointment.

S-Bahn: S 41, S 42, S 8, S 85, S 9
to "Treptower Park"
U-Bahn: U 1 to "Schlesisches Tor"

"Parliament of Trees" / Wall Memorial in the Marie-Elisabeth-Lüders-Haus

The "Parliament of Trees" is situated opposite the Reichstag on Schiffbauerdamm. This memorial against war and violence was set up in the border strip in 1990 by the Berlin artist Ben Wagin and is the work of several artists. The installation, consisting of trees, memorial stones, sculptures and segments of Wall, extends into the Marie-Elisabeth Lüders House, in which the Bundestag library is housed.

"Parlament der Bäume" / Mauermahnmal im Marie-Elisabeth-Lüders-Haus
Promenade Schiffbauerdamm, 10117 Berlin

www.berlin.de / mauer / gedenkstaetten / parlament_der_baeume / index.de.php
www.benwagin.de

Open from Friday to Sunday
11 a.m. – 5 p.m.

Admission free

S-Bahn: S 2 (to S-Bahn station "Unter den Linden")

S 25, S 26, S 3, S 5, S 7
(to "Friedrichstrasse" S-Bahn station)
Bus: Nos. 200, 347
(to "Friedrichstrasse" bus stop)
U-Bahn: U 6 (to "Friedrichstrasse"
U- and S-Bahn station)

East Side Gallery

The East Side Gallery is a 1,300 - metre-long segment of the eastern side of the Wall between Oberbaum Bridge and the Ostbahnhof in Friedrichshain. The largest open-air gallery in the world, it was created in 1990 by over one hundred international artists.

East Side Gallery
Mühlenstrasse, 10243 Berlin

Contact: Künstlerinitiative East Side Gallery e.V., c/o Kani Alavi
Weserstrasse 11, 12047 Berlin

Tel.: +49 (0) 30 - 251 71 59
info@eastsidegallery-berlin.com
www.eastsidegallery-berlin.com
S-Bahn: S 3, S 5, S 7, S 73
("Ostbahnhof" S-Bahn station)
S 5, S 7, S 75 ("Warschauer Strasse")
U-Bahn: U 1 ("Warschauer Strasse")

Berlin Wall Trail (Berliner Mauerweg)

The Berlin Wall Trail runs for 160 kilometres along the course of the former barrier system around West Berlin. The trail, which can be done by bike or on foot, mostly follows the so-called "patrol route" that the GDR border troops built for their guards. For detailed information see: Michael Cramer, Berlin Wall Trail, Rodingersdorf, 7th edition, 2014.
www.berlin.de / mauer / mauerweg

Selected Bibliography

Aanerud, Kai-Axel / Knopp Guido (eds.), 1991: Die eingemauerte Stadt. Die Geschichte der Berliner Mauer, Recklinghausen.

Ahonen, Pertti, 2011: Death at the Berlin Wall, Oxford.

Arnold, Dietmar / Kellerhoff, Sven Felix, 2008: Die Fluchttunnel von Berlin, Berlin.

Ausland, John C., 1996: Kennedy, Khrushchev, and the Berlin-Cuba-Crisis, 1961–1964, Oslo / Boston.

Behrendt, Hans-Dieter, 2003: Im Schatten der "Agentenbrücke". Die Glienicker Brücke – Symbol der deutschen Teilung, Schkeuditz.

Beschloss, Michael R., 1991: The Crisis Years: Kennedy and Khrushchev, 1960–1963, New York.

Beschloss, Michael R. / Talbott, Strobe, 1993: At the Highest Levels: The Inside Story of the End of the Cold War, Boston / Toronto / London [Auf höchster Ebene. Das Ende des Kalten Krieges und die Geheimdiplomatie der Supermächte 1989–1991, Düsseldorf].

Blees, Thomas, 1996: Glienicker Brücke. Ausufernde Geschichten, Berlin.

Bundesministerium für innerdeutsche Beziehungen (ed.), 1986: Der Bau der Mauer durch Berlin. Faksimilierter Nachdruck der Denkschrift von 1961, Bonn.

Cate, Curtis, 1978: The Ides of August: The Berlin Wall Crisis, 1961, New York [Riss durch Berlin. Der 13. August 1961, Hamburg 1980].

Cramer, Michael, 2014: Berlin Wall Trail, Rodingersdorf [Berliner Mauer-Radweg, 7. Aufl., 2014].

Detjen, Marion, 2005: Ein Loch in der Mauer. Die Geschichte der Fluchthilfe im geteilten Deutschland 1961–1989, München.

Diedrich, Torsten / Ehlert, Hans / Wenzke, Rüdiger (eds.), 1998: Im Dienste der Partei. Handbuch der bewaffneten Organe der DDR, Berlin.

Dollmann, Lydia / Wichmann, Manfred (eds.), 2015: Fotografieren verboten! Die Berliner Mauer von Osten gesehen. Mit Aufnahmen und Erinnerungen von Gerd Rücker, Berlin.

Effner, Bettina / Heidemeyer, Helge (eds.), 2005: Flucht im geteilten Deutschland. Erinnerungsstätte Notaufnahmelager Marienfelde, Berlin.

Eisenfeld, Bernd / Engelmann, Roger, 2001: 13.8.1961. Mauerbau. Fluchtbewegung und Machtsicherung, Bremen.

Flemming, Thomas / Koch, Hagen, 1999: Die Berliner Mauer. Geschichte eines politischen Bauwerks, Berlin.

Garton Ash, Timothy, 1993: In Europe's Name, New York [Im Namen Europas. Deutschland und der geteilte Kontinent, München-Wien 1993].

Gelb, Norman, 1986: The Berlin Wall. Kennedy, Krushchev and a Showdown in the Heart of Europe, New York.

Gieseke, Jens, 2014: The History of the Stasi. East Germany's Secret Police, 1945–1990, New York.

Grafe, Roman, 2004: Deutsche Gerechtigkeit. Prozesse gegen DDR-Grenzschützen und ihre Befehlsgeber, München.

Gründer, Ralf, 2007: Verboten: Berliner Mauerkunst, Köln-Weimar-Wien.

Harrison, Hope M., 2003: Driving the Soviets up the Wall. Soviet-East German Relations, 1953–1961, Princeton, N.J. [Ulbrichts Mauer. Wie die SED Moskaus Widerstand gegen den Mauerbau brach, Berlin 2011].

Heidemeyer, Helge, 1994: Flucht und Zuwanderung aus der SBZ/DDR 1945/1949–1961, Düsseldorf.

Henke, Klaus-Dietmar (ed.), 2011: Die Mauer. Errichtung – Überwindung – Erinnerung, München.

Hertle, Hans-Hermann, 1999: Der Fall der Mauer. Die unbeabsichtigte Selbstauflösung des SED-Staates, 2. Aufl., Opladen/Wiesbaden.

Hertle, Hans-Hermann, 2009: Chronik des Mauerfalls. Die dramatischen Ereignisse um den 9. November 1989, 12. Aufl., Berlin.

Hertle, Hans-Hermann/Elsner, Kathrin, 2009: Der Tag, an dem die Mauer fiel, Berlin.

Hertle, Hans-Hermann/Jarausch, Konrad H./Kleßmann, Christoph (eds.), 2002: Vom Mauerbau zum Mauerfall. Ursachen – Verlauf – Auswirkungen, Berlin.

Hertle, Hans-Hermann/Jarausch, Konrad H. (eds.), 2006: Risse im Bruderbund. Die Gespräche Honecker – Breshnew, Berlin.

Hertle, Hans-Hermann/Nooke, Maria (eds.), 2009: Die Todesopfer an der Berliner Mauer. Ein biographisches Handbuch, 2. Aufl., Berlin [The Victims at the Berlin Wall. A Biographical Handbook, Berlin 2011].

Hildebrandt, Alexandra, 2001: Die Mauer. Zahlen, Daten, Berlin.

Hildebrandt, Rainer, 2004: Es geschah an der Mauer / It happened at the Wall / Cela s'est passé au mur, 21. Aufl., Berlin.

Hollitzer, Tobias/Bohse, Reinhard (eds.), 2000: Heute vor 10 Jahren. Leipzig auf dem Weg zur friedlichen Revolution, Fribourg.

"Im Politbüro des ZK der KPdSU …". Nach Aufzeichnungen von Anatolij Tschernajew, Wadim Medwedew und Georgij Schachnasarow, Moskau 2006 (in Russian).

Jarausch, Konrad H., 1994: The Rush to German Unity, New York [Die unverhoffte Einheit 1989/90, Frankfurt am Main 1995].

Kaminsky, Anna/Gleinig, Ruth/Heidenreich, Ronny, 2014: Die Berliner Mauer in der Welt, hg. im Auftrag der Bundesstiftung zur Aufarbeitung der SED-Diktatur, Berlin, 2. Aufl.

Klausmeier, Axel (ed.), 2015: The Berlin Wall Memorial, Berlin.

Klausmeier, Axel/Schmidt, Leo, 2004: Mauerreste – Mauerspuren. Der umfassende Führer zur Berliner Mauer, Berlin [Wall Remnants — Wall Traces. The Comprehensive Guide to the Berlin Wall, Berlin-Bonn 2004].

Knabe, Hubertus (ed.), 2009: Die vergessenen Opfer der Mauer. Inhaftierte DDR-Flüchtlinge berichten, Berlin.

Koop, Volker, 1996: "Den Gegner vernichten". Die Grenzsicherung der DDR, Bonn.

Kowalczuk, Ilko-Sascha, 2009: Endspiel. Die Revolution von 1989 in der DDR, München.

Kraus, Dorothea, 2015: Tränenpalast. Ort der deutschen Teilung, hg. v. Stiftung

Haus der Geschichte der Bundesrepublik Deutschland, Bonn.

Kuhlmann, Bernd, 1998: Züge durch Mauer und Stacheldraht, Berlin.

Kunze, Gerhard, 1999: Grenzerfahrungen. Kontakte und Verhandlungen zwischen dem Land Berlin und der DDR 1949–1989, Berlin.

Laabs, Rainer / Sikorski, Werner, 1997: Checkpoint Charlie und die Mauer. Ein geteiltes Volk wehrt sich, Berlin [Checkpoint Charlie and the Wall. A Divided People Rebel, Berlin].

Lapp, Peter Joachim, 1999: Gefechtsdienst im Frieden. Das Grenzregime der DDR 1945–1990, Bonn.

Lapp, Peter Joachim / Ritter, Jürgen, 2011: Die Grenze. Ein deutsches Bauwerk, 8. Aufl., Berlin.

Marxen, Klaus / Werle, Gerhard (eds.), 2002: Strafjustiz und DDR-Unrecht. Dokumentation, 2 Bde., 2. Teilband: Gewalttaten an der deutsch-deutschen Grenze, Berlin.

Marxen, Klaus / Werle, Gerhard / Schäfter, Petra, 2007: Die Strafverfolgung von DDR-Unrecht. Fakten und Zahlen, Berlin.

Maurer, Jochen, 2015: Halt – Staatsgrenze! Alltag, Dienst und Innenansichten der Grenztruppen der DDR, Berlin.

Müller, Bodo, 2013: Faszination Freiheit. Die spektakulärsten Fluchtgeschichten, 6. Aufl., Berlin.

Neubert, Ehrhart, 2008: Unsere Revolution. Die Geschichte der Jahre 1989 / 90, München.

Nooke, Maria, 2002: Der verratene Tunnel. Geschichte einer verhinderten Flucht im geteilten Berlin, Bremen.

Nooke, Maria / Dollmann, Lydia (eds.), 2011: Fluchtziel Freiheit. Berichte von DDR-Flüchtlingen über die Situation nach dem Mauerbau, Berlin.

Oplatka, Andreas, 2009: Der erste Riss in der Mauer. September 1989 – Ungarn öffnet die Grenze, Wien.

Petschull, Jürgen, 1990: Die Mauer. August 1961. Zwölf Tage zwischen Krieg und Frieden, 3. Aufl., Hamburg.

Plato, Alexander von, 2009: Die Vereinigung Deutschlands – ein weltpolitisches Macht-spiel, 3. Aufl., Berlin.

Pond, Elizabeth, 1993: Beyond the Wall. Germany's Road to Unification, Washington, D.C.

Rathje, Wolfgang, 2001: "Mauer-Marketing" unter Erich Honecker, Kiel.

Rehlinger, Ludwig A., 1991: Freikauf. Die Geschäfte der DDR mit politisch Verfolgten 1963–1989, Berlin / Frankfurt a. M.

Rühle, Jürgen / Holzweißig Gunter (eds.), 1988: 13. August 1961. Die Mauer von Berlin, 3. Aufl., Köln.

Rummler, Thoralf, 2000: Die Gewalttaten an der deutsch-deutschen Grenze vor Gericht, Baden-Baden.

Sälter, Gerhard, 2004: Der Abbau der Berliner Mauer und noch sichtbare Reste in der Berliner Innenstadt, Berlin.

Sarotte, Mary E., 2009: 1989. The Struggle to Create Post-Cold War Europe, Princeton.

Sarotte, Mary E., 2014: The Collapse. The Accidental Opening of the Berlin Wall, New York.

Sauer, Heiner / Plumeyer, Hans-Otto, 1991: Der Salzgitter Report. Die Zentrale Erfassungsstelle berichtet über Verbrechen im SED-Staat, München.

Schnell, Gabriele, 2009: Das "Lindenhotel". Berichte aus dem Potsdamer Geheimdienstgefängnis, 3. Aufl., Berlin.

Schroeder, Klaus, 2013: Der SED-Staat. Geschichte und Strukturen der DDR 1949–1990, Köln.

Schuller, Wolfgang, 2009: Die deutsche Revolution 1989, Berlin.

Schultke, Dietmar, 2000: "Keiner kommt durch". Die Geschichte der innerdeutschen Grenze 1945–1990, 2. Aufl., Berlin.

Schumann, Karl F. u. a., 1996: Private Wege der Wiedervereinigung. Die deutsche Ost-West-Migration vor der Wende, Weinheim.

Sesta, Ellen, 2001: Der Tunnel in die Freiheit, München.

Steiner, André, 2010: The Plans That Failed. An Economic History of East Germany, 1945–1989, New York / Oxford.

Steininger, Rolf, 2009: Berlinkrise und Mauerbau 1958 bis 1963, 4. erw. Aufl., München.

Taylor, Frederick, 2006: The Berlin Wall: 13 August 1961 – 9 November 1989, London [Die Mauer. 13. August 1961 bis 9. November 1989, Berlin 2009].

Tusa, Ann, 1996: The Last Division. Berlin and the Wall, London.

Uhl, Matthias, 2008: Krieg um Berlin? Die sowjetische Militär- und Sicherheitspolitik in der zweiten Berlin-Krise 1958 bis 1962, München.

Uhl, Matthias / Wagner, Armin (eds.), 2003: Ulbricht, Chruschtschow und die Mauer. Eine Dokumentation, München.

Wagner, Armin, 2002: Walter Ulbricht und die geheime Sicherheitspolitik der SED, Berlin.

Weidenfeld, Werner (mit Peter Wagner und Elke Bruck), 1998: Außenpolitik für die deutsche Einheit: Die Entscheidungsjahre 1989 / 90, Stuttgart.

Wettig, Gerhard, 2006: Chruschtschows Berlin-Krise, 1958–1963, München.

Wettig, Gerhard, 2011: Chruschtschows Westpolitik 1955 – 1964, München.

Whitney, Craig R., 1993: Advocatus Diaboli: Wolfgang Vogel – Anwalt zwischen Ost und West. Berlin.

Wilke, Manfred, 2011: Der Weg zur Mauer: Stationen der Teilungsgeschichte, Berlin.

Wölbern, Jan Philipp, 2014: Der Häftlingsfreikauf aus der DDR 1962/63 –1989 – Zwischen Menschenhandel und humanitären Aktionen, Göttingen.

Wolle, Stefan, 2009: Die heile Welt der Diktatur. Alltag und Herrschaft in der DDR 1971 –1989, 3. Aufl., Berlin.

Wyden, Peter, 1989: Wall. The Inside Story of Divided Berlin, New York 1989 [Die Mauer war unser Schicksal, Berlin 1995].

Zelikow, Philip / Rice, Condoleezza, 1995: Germany Unified and Europe Transformed, Boston [Sternstunde der Diplomatie. Die deutsche Einheit und das Ende der Spaltung Europas, Berlin 1997].

Notes

1/ Where the Wall stood

p. 23 Figures on the Berlin Wall, see: *"Auskunft zum Grenzkommando-Mitte und der Staatsgrenze der DDR zu Westberlin,"* Streng Geheim (March 1989), and *"Sicherung der Staatsgrenze im Bezirk Potsdam,"* 12 May 1989, in: BStU, MfS, Büro Neiber Nr. 60; Der Polizeipräsident in Berlin [PHS].

2 / Before the Wall went up

p. 31 Churchill quote, see: Robert R. James, *Winston S. Churchill: His Complete Speeches 1897–1963*, Vol. VII: 1943–1949, New York/London 1974, pp. 7285–7293.

p. 34 Escapee reports: BMiB 1986, p. 64; Escape statistics: *Monatsmeldungen des Bundesministeriums für Vertriebene, Flüchtlinge und Kriegsgeschädigte*, doc. in: Rühle/Holzweißig 1988, p. 154.

p. 35 Mikojan quote in: SAPMO-BA, DY 30/J IV 2/2/766. **p. 36** f. On the Berlin crisis 1958–1963, see: Ausland 1996, Steininger 2001, Eisenfeld/Engelmann 2001, Harrison 2003, Uhl/Wagner 2003, Wettig 2006. **p. 37** Khrushchev quote in: Hans Kroll, *Lebenserinnerungen eines Botschafters*, Berlin 1967, p. 512. **p. 39** Quotes from Walter Ulbricht's international press conference in: *Dokumente zur Deutschlandpolitik*, IV/6 (1961), pp. 925 ff.

3 / Building the Wall

p. 44 Quote from East Berlin doctor in: BA, B 285/389, Nr. 17503, 22.8.1961.

p. 45 Quote from GDR Council of Ministers in: Rühle/Holzweißig 1988, p. 95; Senate

communiqué quote: *Bulletin des Presse- und Informationsamtes der Bundesregierung* No. 150, 15. August 1961, p. 1455; Messmer quote: interview by the author with Pierre Messmer, 13 March 2001 (TNM documentary *Mauerbau*); Kissinger quote: interview by the author with Henry Kissinger, 20 April 2001 (TNM documentary *Mauerbau*).

p. 48 On Conrad Schumann: Der Polizeipräsident in Berlin, Vermerk über gesprächsweise Abhörung eines Überläufers der Bereitschaftspolizei am 15.8.1961 bei der Polizeiinspektion Wedding, Berlin, 16.8.1961 [PHS]; *Süddeutsche Zeitung*, 14./15.8.1991; WDR 5, *Bilder im Kopf*, 5.2.2007.

p. 49 Wesner quote: interview by the author with Lothar Wesner, 2 April 2001 (TNM documentary *Mauerbau*). **p. 50** Brandt quote: Speech by the Governing Mayor of Berlin, Brandt, at a rally in Berlin, 16 August 1961, in: *Dokumente zur Deutschlandpolitik*, IV/7 (1961) p. 53. **p. 51** Kennedy quote to Brandt, 18 August 1961: U.S. Department of State (ed.), *Foreign Relations of the United States, Vol. XV: Berlin Crisis, 1962–1963*, Washington 1994, pp. 345/46; Kennedy quote to Johnson: letter from President Kennedy to Vice-President Johnson, 18 August 1961, cited in: Petschull 1990, doc. 11, p. 233; Johnson quote, 19 August 1961: speech by Vice-President Johnson at a rally in Berlin, 19 August 1961, in: *Dokumente zur Deutschlandpolitik*, IV/7 (1961), p. 150.

p. 52 Johnson quote, 21.8.1961: memorandum from Vice-President Johnson to President Kennedy, 21 August 1961, cited in: Petschull 1990, doc. 16, p. 249.

p. 53 SED Politbüro quote in: Protokoll Nr. 45/61 der Sitzung des Politbüros des ZK der SED im Sitzungssaal des Politbüros,

22 August 1961, in: SAPMO-BA, DY 30/J IV 2/2/787, p. 1 f.; on the murder of Günter Litfin, see: Jürgen Litfin, *Tod durch fremde Hand. Das erste Maueropfer in Berlin und die Geschichte einer Familie,* Husum 2006; Christine Brecht in: Hertle/Nooke (eds.) 2011, pp. 39–41. **p. 56** Schaar quote: interview by Ulrich Kasten with Monika Schaar, 11 March 2001 (TNM documentary *Mauerbau*). **p. 63** On "Last train to freedom", see: Tätigkeitsbericht des S für den Monat Dezember 1961, Berlin, 5.1.1962 [PHS]; Kuhlmann 1998, pp. 16–22; Müller 2008, pp. 10–27. **p. 64** Mielke quote in: BStU, MfS, SdM Nr. 1558, p. 36; Laetsch quote in: interview by Ullrich Kasten with Helmut Laetsch, 26 February 2001 (TNM documentary *Mauerbau*)

4 / Escapes / Escape Helpers / Resistance

p. 68 On escape aid in general, see: Detjen 2005. **p. 70** "Successful escapes": Ritter/Lapp 2011, p. 176 and 180, and: *Flüchtlinge seit dem 13.8.1961 gemäß polizeilicher Feststellungen (Jahresangaben nach der "Mauerstatistik" der Berliner Polizei),* 28.10.1986 [PHS]. **p. 72** On the murder of Dieter Wohlfahrt, see: BStU, Ast. Potsdam, AU 1753/62; *Der Spiegel* No. 13, 28.3.1962, pp. 54/55; Christine Brecht in: Hertle/Nooke (eds.) 2011, pp. 62–64. **p. 74** On escape by tunnels in general, see: Arnold/Kellerhoff 2008; "Senior citizens' tunnel": *Der Tagesspiegel,* 19.5.1962. **p. 77** "Tunnel 29": Sesta 2001. **p. 78** "Tunnel 57": Müller 2008, pp. 75–102. **p. 80** Lazai quote: Hans-Joachim Lazai, "Widerstand gegen die Mauer. Der Anschlag vom 26. Mai 1962," in: Hinckeldey-Stiftung (ed.), *Berliner Polizei. Von 1945 bis zur Gegenwart,* Berlin 1998, pp. 80/81; "Die Gewalt der anderen Seite hat mich sehr

getroffen." Interview by Doris Liebermann with Hans-Joachim Lazai, in: *Deutschland Archiv* 4/2006, pp. 596–607. **p. 83** On the reconstruction of Peter Fechter's death see the investigative television feature by Heribert Schwan, *Ein gewisser Peter Fechter,* ARD documentary, WDR Köln 1997; Christine Brecht in: Hertle/Nooke (eds.) 2011, pp. 102–105. **p. 84** Engels quote: interview by the author with Wolfgang Engels, doc. in: Jürgen Wetzel (ed.), *Berlin in Geschichte und Gegenwart. Jahrbuch des Landesarchivs Berlin 2003,* Berlin 2003, p. 164. **p. 85** Bus escape: Hans-Hermann Hertle/Sven-Felix Kellerhoff, "Ein Meter fehlte bis zur Freiheit," in: *Berliner Morgenpost,* 13.8.2007. **p. 87** Escape by bulldozer: Lagemeldung der West-Berliner Polizei, 12 September 1966 [PHS]; *Die Welt,* 12 September 1966; *BZ,* 12 September 1966; *Der Tagesspiegel,* 13 September 1966. **p. 89** "Trojan cow": Interview by Peter Böger with Angelika B. and her husband, 15 November 2004 (Name altered); BStU, Ast. Potsdam, AU 493/70.

5 / Confrontation and Détente

p. 92 The masterminds behind the "policy of small steps" and "change through rapprochement" were Willy Brandt and Egon Bahr. From their point of view, see: Egon Bahr, *Zu meiner Zeit,* Munich 1996. **p. 93** Kennedy speech card: reproduced with kind permission of the John F. Kennedy Presidential Library. **p. 95** Khrushchev quote: Prime Minister Khrushchev's speech at the fourth SED party congress, 16 January 1963, in: *Dokumente zur Deutschlandpolitik,* IV/9 (1963), p. 41; Kennedy quote: President Kennedy's speech at the Freie Universität, 26 June 1963, in: *Dokumente zur Deutschlandpolitik,* IV/9

(1963), p. 465. **p. 99** On ransoming prisoners in general, see: Rehlinger 1991, Whitney 1993. **p. 100** On negotiating the border-pass agreement, see: Kunze 1999. **p. 102** Brandt quote: Willy Brandt, *Erinnerungen*, 4th ed., Berlin/Frankfurt a.M. 1990, p. 226; Brezhnev quoted in: Hertle/ Wolle 2004, p. 162; Honecker quoted in: Hertle 1999, p. 26.

6 / Perfecting the Border Barrier System

p. 106 On fortifying the barrier system, see: Rathje 2001; quote National Defence Council: Protokoll der 12. Sitzung des NVR der DDR, 12 September 1962. **p. 110** On the different generations of the Wall, see: Klausmeier/ Schmidt 2004, pp. 14–17. **p. 116/17** Costs of the border system up to 1970, see: Stadtkommandant der Hauptstadt der DDR/ Generalmajor Poppe, "Kostenberechnung für den Ausbau des Grenzsicherungsstreifens entlang der Staatsgrenze zu Westberlin in der Zeit von 1966–1970," Anlage 3 zur Vorlage Nr. 14/65, doc. in: Rathje 2001, pp. 1394/95. **p. 117** On the staffing levels of the armed forces in the GDR, see articles in: Diedrich/Ehlert/Wenzke 1998. **p. 118** Information on Central Border Command, see: *"Auskunft zum Grenzkommando-Mitte (GK-Mitte) und der Staatsgrenze der DDR zu Westberlin,"* Streng Geheim (March 1989), and "Sicherung der Staatsgrenze im Bezirk Potsdam," 12 May 1989, in: BStU, MfS, Büro Neiber Nr. 60; on the history of the border troops, see: Lapp 1999; Schultke 2000. **p. 119** On the "Berlin Grouping" and its task of capturing West Berlin, see: Oberst i.G. Hoffmann, *Korps- und Territorialkommando Ost/IV. Korps, Die Besetzung West-Berlins*, manuscript, not dated (1993), p. 2, **p. 120** On the use of firearms in the border region,

see: Anklageschrift der Staatsanwaltschaft bei dem Kammergericht Berlin gegen Erich Honecker u.a., 12 May 1992 (2 Js 26/90), particularly pp. 298–330. **p. 121** Oral command ("Vergatterung"): MfNV, DV 30/10: *Organisation und Führung der Grenzsicherung in der Grenzkompanie*, 1967, VVS Nr. A 20367, p. 43; Honecker quote 1974: Protokoll der 45. Sitzung des NVR der DDR, 3 May 1974, in: BA, DVW 1/39503, Bl. 34; Hoffmann quote: *Armee-filmschau* 7/1966; Honecker quote 1989: *"Niederschrift über die Rücksprache beim Minister für Nationale Verteidigung, i.V. Generaloberst Streletz, am 3. April 1989"* [BStU, MfS, HA I Nr. 5753].

7 / Deaths at the Berlin Wall

p. 124 The figures and the list of deaths at the Berlin Wall are based on: Hertle/Nooke (eds.) 2011; see also: Ahonen 2011.

8 / The Wall in the Honecker Era, 1971–1989

p. 136 On the expansion of the MfS in the Honecker era, see: Gieseke 2014. **p. 139** Visits and permanent departure, see: Hertle 2009, pp. 46–51; Escape aid in the 1970s and 1980s, see: Detjen 2005, pp. 270 f. **p. 140** Hartmut Richter: Text by Gabriele Schnell on the basis of the following descriptions: exhibition of the Marienfelde Refugee Center Musuem; Stiftung Gedenkstätte Berlin-Hohenschönhausen 2003, pp. 49–51; Matthias Bath, "Die Fluchthelfer Rainer Schubert und Hartmut Richter," in: *Wege nach Bautzen II. Biographische und autobiographische Porträts, eingeleitet von Silke Klewin und Kirsten Wenzel*, Dresden 1998. **p. 143** Table of payments for the ransom of political prisoners, see: Whitney

1993, p. 400. **p. 145** On relations between the GDR and the Soviet Union up to 1982, see: Hertle/Jarausch 2006. **p. 147** On the emigration movement, see: Eisenfeld 1999, pp. 381–421, and Hertle 1999, pp. 80–91; quotes and sources are also taken from these sources. **p. 149** Table of applications for departure, see: Bernd Eisenfeld, "Flucht und Ausreise – Macht und Ohnmacht," in: Eberhard Kuhrt/Hansjörg F. Buck/Gunter Holzweißig (eds.), *Opposition in der DDR von den 70er Jahren bis zum Zusammenbruch der SED-Herrschaft,* Opladen 1999, p. 400. **p. 150** Gisela Lotz: text by Gabriele Schnell, see also: Gabriele Schnell, *Das "Lindenhotel". Berichte aus dem Potsdamer Geheimdienstgefängnis,* 3rd ed., Berlin 2009, pp. 157–169. **p. 153** Jäger quote: Hertle 1999, pp. 380/81. **p. 156** Jäger quote: Hertle 1999, p. 380. **p. 158** Glienicke Bridge, see: Kunze 1999, Blees 1996, Behrendt 2003.

p. 160 On radioactive border checks, see: Hans Halter, "Es gibt kein Entrinnen," in: *Der Spiegel* No. 51, 10 December 1994, pp. 176–180; Strahlenrisiko durch ehemalige DDR-Grenzkontrollen mittels Cs-137-Strahlung. Stellungnahme der Strahlenschutzkommission, 17 February 1995.

p. 161 Powered glider, 20 December 1986: BStU, MfS, AGM Nr. 480, Bl. 267–269.

p. 162 Light plane, 15 July 1987: *Der Tagesspiegel,* 16 July 1987; *Die Welt,* 16 July 1987.

p. 163 Failed car escape, 9 December 1987: BStU, MfS, HA VI 158. **p. 164** Successful truck escape, 10 March 1988, see: Strehlow 2004, pp. 68–75; BStU, MfS, HA VI Nr. 158, Nr. 10101; BStU, Ast. Potsdam, AKG Nr. 868; BStU, Ast. Potsdam, Abt. IX Nr. 122; *Der Tagesspiegel,* 11 March 1988; *Die Welt,* 11 March 1988; *Berliner Morgenpost,*

11 March 1988. **p. 165** Failed car escape, 29 June 1989: BStU, MfS, HA VI Nr. 119.

p. 167 Gorbachev quote 27 March 1986: *Im Politbüro des ZK der KPdSU …* 2006. **p. 170** Gorbachev quote late 1986, see: SAPMO-BA, DY 30/IV 2/1/658. **p. 172** quote Gorbachev 1986. **p. 173** Reagan quote 12 June 1987: President Reagan's speech at the Brandenburg Gate, 12 June 1987, in: Helmut Trotnow/Florian Weiß (eds.), *Tear Down this Wall. US-Präsident Ronald Reagan vor dem Brandenburger Tor, 12. Juni 1987,* Berlin 2007, p. 218;

p. 174 Honecker quote June 1988, see HA XVIII/4, Information [über die Beratung im Politbüro am 14. Juni 1988] von Major Friedrich an Generalmajor Alfred Kleine, 16 June 1988 [BStU, MfS, HA XVIII Nr. 3376, Bl. 47]; Mittag quote November 1988, see: Heinz Klopfer, Persönliche Notizen über ein Gespräch beim Mitglied des Politbüros und Sekretär des ZK der SED, Genossen Dr. Günter Mittag, 23 November 1988 [BStU, MfS, HA XVIII Nr. 3374, Bl. 118].

p. 175 Honecker quote in: *Neues Deutschland,* 20 January 1989.

9 / The Fall of the Wall

p. 178 On the run-up and background to the fall of the Wall and German unity in general, see: Beschloss/Talbott 1993; Garton Ash 1993; Hertle 1999, pp. 87 f.; Hertle 2009, pp. 62 f.; Jarausch 1994; Kowalczuk 2009; Neubert 2009; von Plato 2002; Sarotte 2009; Sarotte 2014; Schuller 2009; Weidenfeld 1998; Zelikow/Rice 1995; Honecker quote: *Neues Deutschland,* 20 January 1989; on the murder of Chris Gueffroy, see: Udo Baron/Hans-Hermann Hertle in: Hertle/Nooke (eds.) 2011, pp. 423–27; on Winfried Freudenberg, see:

Martin Ahrends/Udo Baron/Hans-Hermann Hertle in: Hertle/Nooke (eds.) 2011, pp. 428–31. **p. 180** Failed escape at Chausseestraße border crossing: BStU, MfS, HA VI Nr. 10101; *Die Welt,* 10 April 1989; *Der Tagesspiegel,* 11 April 1989; Bert G. quote: *Berliner Morgenpost,* 3 January 1993; Honecker quote on the repeal of the order to shoot, 3 April 1989, see: BStU, MfS, HA I Nr. 5753. **p. 187** On Leipzig, see: Hollitzer/Bohse 2000. **p. 188** "Analyse zur ökonomischen Lage der DDR," doc. in: Hertle 1999, pp. 448 f.. **p. 190** Kohl quote: Deutscher Bundestag, 11. Wahlperiode, 173. Sitzung, 8 November 1989, stenographic report, p. 13017; Krenz quote: Hertle/Stephan 1999, p. 303. **p. 193** Schabowski quote: Hertle/Elsner 2009, p. 44. **p. 194/95** Text of the press conference: transcript by the author of an audio-visual recording of the press conference on 9 November 1989.

p. 197 "We're opening the floodgates now," cited in: Hertle 2009, p. 166; quote on the Invalidenstraße border crossing: Hertle/Elsner 2009, pp. 150–152. **p. 202** Conny Hansch-mann quote: Hertle/Elsner 2009, p. 188.

p. 204 Teltschik quote: Horst Teltschik, *329 Tage. Innenansichten der Einigung,* Berlin 1991, p. 23. **p. 206** NVA commander quote: Hertle 2009, p. 260. **p. 208/209** Weizsäcker quote: Hertle/Elsner 2009, p. 260/261.

p. 216 George Bush quote: Hertle/Elsner 2009, p. 238; Mikhail Gorbachev quote: Hertle/Elsner 2009, pp. 246/47.

p. 217 Helmut Kohl quote: Hertle/Elsner 2009, pp. 245/46. **p. 218** On criminal prosecutions, see: Bernhard Jahntz, *Die Bilanz der Strafverfolgung des SED-Unrechts,* presentation manuscript, Wustrau 2007; Schwerpunktabteilung der Staatsanwalt-

schaft Neuruppin für Bezirkskriminalität und DDR-Justizunrecht, Bilanz 2006; see also: Rummler 2000, Marxen/Werle 2002, Grafe 2004, Marxen/Werle/Schäfter 2007.

p.222 On the demolition of the Wall, see also: Sälter 2004. **p. 225** Berlin Wall in tonnes: Peter Thomsen, "Der Abbau der Sperranlagen an der ehemaligen Berliner Grenze," in: *Vom Mauerbau zum Mauerfall, Teil 1,* ed. Brandenburger Verein für politische Bildung "Rosa Luxemburg" e.V., Potsdam 1997, pp. 31/32.

Appendix/Service

p. 228 Revised by Gabriele Schnell. For detailed information on museums, memorial sites and other sites of remembrance, see the websites of the Berlin Senate www.berlin.de/mauer/index.de.html and of the Federal Foundation for the Reappraisal of the SED Dictatorship www.stiftung-aufarbeitung.de Many thanks to Transfer Film Neue Medien GmbH (TNM) and Cine Impuls Film und Video KG for permission to use interviews carried out for two ARD documentaries: *It happend in August. The Building of the Berlin Wall/Es geschah im August. Der Bau der Berliner Mauer* (TNM/SFB et al. 2001; authors: Ullrich Kasten and Hans-Hermann Hertle) and *When the Wall Came Tumbling Down – 50 Hours That Changed the World/Als die Mauer fiel – 50 Stunden, die die Welt veränderten* (Cine Impuls/SFB et al. 1999; authors: Gunther Scholz and Hans-Hermann Hertle).

Photo Sources

l = left, r = right, t = top, b = bottom,
c = center

AKG: 169b, 183

AP: 180, 181, 182

Jürgen Ast Film- und Videoproduktion: 142

Axel Springer AG/Ullstein GmbH: 122
(Cetin Mert)

Hans-Dieter Behrendt: 158, 159t, 162

Berliner Mauer-Archiv Hagen Koch:
17, 19, 53r, 112, 114/15, 119, 132/33, 219

Bildarchiv Preußischer Kulturbesitz: 61

BStU: 69, 72, 75, 88, 89, 120, 122
(Hildegard Trabant; Winfried Freudenberg),
141, 153, 154, 155, 157, 159b, 161, 163,
164, 165, 221

Bundesarchiv: 35 (183-57000-0138/Sturm),
36 (183-83494-0010), 38 (183-83911-009),
43 (183-85458-0001/Junge), 69b (183-
1990-0720-302/Kull), 94b (146-2006-
0069/Jurisch), 97c (183-K1102-032/
Franke), 97b (183-L0614-040/Koard),
107b (B 145 Bild-P091010), 117 (183-
E0813-0027-0001), 168t (183-1986-1012-
009/Koard), 172 (183-1986-0416-418/
Reiche), 174 (183-1989-0119-042),
186 (183-1989-1007-402),
190 (183-1989-1108-406), 194 (183-
1989-1109-030/Lehmann), 224t (183-
1990-0508-421/Kull)

Deutsches Historisches Museum: 24/25

Deutsches Rundfunk-Archiv: 192

DPA-Alliance: 189, 191b, 217

Erinnerungsstätte Notaufnahmelager
Marienfelde: 33, 138

Gerhard Gäbler: 187

Gedenkstätte Berliner Mauer: 78, 79

Hans-Hermann Hertle: 10/11, 20, 98, 151,
226, 227

John F. Kennedy Library: 93

Hilde Kroll: 224b, 225

Landesarchiv Berlin: 56 (LAB/Horst Sieg-
mann, F Rep. 290, Nr. 78184),
57b (LAB/Horst Siegmann, F Rep. 290,
Nr. 77247), 59 (LAB/Horst Siegmann,
F Rep. 290, Nr. 77058), 60 (LAB/W. Schäfer,
F Rep. 290, Nr. C 1163), 86 (LAB/J. Jung,
F Rep. 290, Nr. 102921), 90/91 (LAB/Bert
Sass, F Rep. 290, Nr. C 1108)

Gisela Lotz: 150

Dajana Marquardt: 12, 14, 16t, 17t, 18t, 19t

Polizeihistorische Sammlung des Polizeipräsidenten in Berlin: 2, 21, 48, 50, 52, 62,
63, 73, 76, 77, 81, 82, 85, 87, 96b, 96c,
97t, 107, 109, 110, 111

Potsdam Museum: 27

Presse- und Informationsamt der
Bundesregierung: 43, 49, 54, 94t, 96t,
104/105, 146, 168c, 168b, 169t, 184, 191,
200/201, 202/203, 208, 209, 212, 215, 223

Presse- und Informationsamt des Senats
von Berlin: 22

Privately owned: 53l (Günter Litfin), 122/123
(Günter Litfin, Hans Räwel, Michael Kollender,
Eduard Wroblewski, Karl-Heinz Kube,
Giuseppe Savoca, Herbert Kiebler,
Ulrich Steinhauer, Marienetta Jirkowsky,
Rainer Liebeke, Lutz Schmidt, Chris Gueffroy);
179r (Chris Gueffroy)

Thomas Raupach/Argus: 211

Jürgen Ritter: 137

Andreas Schoelzel: 176/177

Spiegel-TV: 198/199

Spiegel-Verlag: 160

Staatsarchiv Hamburg: 46/47
(Sign.: STAH CP 32512/Peter Leibing)

Stiftung Haus der Geschichte der
Bundesrepublik Deutschland: 28/29
(1987/3/061)

Ullstein Bild: 40/41, 44, 55, 57t, 58, 65,
66/67, 74, 83, 84, 101, 108, 145, 205, 206

Many thanks to all license-holders for kindly
providing printing permission. Fees may still
be granted in cases in which it proved
impossible to establish the right holders.

Acknowledgements

For their expert and dedicated support for
my picture and document research and
their helpful suggestions and critical advice,
I would like to thank: Jürgen and Daniel Ast,
Udo Baron, Karl-Heinz Baum, Peter Böger,
Hildegard Bremer, Arvid Brunnemann,
Wolfgang Borkmann, Christine Brecht,
Gabriele Camphausen, Klaus Deutschländer,
Bettina Effner, Roger Engelmann,
Stefan Falk, Bärbel Fest, Sylvia Gräfe,
Lucia Halder, Hope M. Harrison,
Doris Hauschke, Helge Heidemeyer,
Bernhard Jahntz, Bernd Keichel-Enders,
Sven Felix Kellerhoff, Hagen Koch,
Hilde Kroll, Christoph Links, Maria Nooke,
Claudia Promnitz, Wolfgang Rathje,
Annelie Rosenmueller, Ekkehard Runge,
Gerhard Sälter, Mary E. Sarotte,
Gabriele Schnell, Hannelore Strehlow,
Berit Walter, Hans-Werner Weber and
Hannes Wittenberg.

I'd also like to thank Sabine Berthold, Birte
Lock, Egbert Meyer, Michael Schultheiss
and Thorsten Schilling for their excellent
work on the editorial team for the website
www.chronik-der-mauer.de.

Abbreviations

Abt. Abteilung / department

ADN Allgemeiner Deutscher Nachrichtendienst / East German press agency

AKG Auswertungs- und Kontrollgruppe (Stasi) / evaluation and control group

AP Associated Press

ARD Arbeitsgemeinschaft der öffentlich-rechtlichen Rundfunkanstalten der Bundesrepublik Deutschland / consortium of public-law broadcasting institutions of the Federal Republic of Germany

ASt. Außenstelle / branch office

AZN Archiv-Zugangsnummer / archive access number

BA Bundesarchiv / Federal Archives

BMiB Bundesministerium für innerdeutsche Beziehungen / Federal Ministry of Inner-German Affairs (West German)

BRD Bundesrepublik Deutschland / Federal Republic of Germany (West Germany)

BStU Der Bundesbeauftragte für die Unterlagen des Ministeriums für Staatssicherheit der ehemaligen DDR / Federal Commissioner for the Records of the State Security Service of the former German Democratic Republic

BV/BVfS Bezirksverwaltung für Staatssicherheit / District Administration for State Security

CC Central Committee

CDU Christlich-Demokratische Union Deutschlands / Christian Democratic Union (West German)

CIA Central Intelligence Agency

CPSU Communist Party of the Soviet Union

Cs Caesium

CSCE Conference on Security and Cooperation in Europe

DDR Deutsche Demokratische Republik / German Democratic Republic (East Germany)

DM Deutsche Mark (West German currency)

doc. document

DPA Deutsche Presse Agentur / German Press Agency (West German)

DRA Deutsches Rundfunkarchiv / German Broadcasting Archive

FDJ Freie Deutsche Jugend / Free German Youth (East German)

FRG Federal Republic of Germany (West Germany)

GDR German Democratic Republic (East Germany)

GK Grenzkommando / border command

GR Grenzregiment / border regiment

GT Grenztruppen / border troops

GTÜ Grenztruppen-Überlieferung / border troops files

GÜST Grenzübergangsstelle / border crossing

GVS Geheime Verschlußsache / strictly confidential

HA Hauptabteilung / central department

KGB Komitet Gosudarstvennoy Bezopasnosti (Soviet secret police)

LAB Landesarchiv Berlin / State Archive of Berlin

MA Militärarchiv / military archive

MdI Ministerium des Innern / Ministry of Interior (East German)

MfNV Ministerium für Nationale Verteidigung / Ministry for National Defence (East German)

MfS Ministerium für Staatssicherheit / Ministry for State Security (i.e. Stasi, East German)

MR Ministerrat / Council of Ministers (East German)

NATO North Atlantic Treaty Organization

NVA Nationale Volksarmee / National People's Army (East German)

NVR Nationaler Verteidigungsrat / National Defence Council (East German)

PB Politbüro / Politburo

PHS Polizeihistorische Sammlung des Polizeipräsidenten in Berlin / Police Historical Collection of the Berlin Police President

RIAS Radio in the American Sector (West Berlin)

SAPMO Stiftung Archiv der Parteien und Massenorganisationen der DDR / Foundation Archive of Parties and Mass Organizations of East Germany

SBZ Sowjetische Besatzungszone / Soviet Zone of Occupation

SdM Sekretariat des Ministers / Minister's Secretariat (Stasi)

SED Sozialistische Einheitspartei Deutschlands / Socialist Unity Party (Communist Party in East Germany)

SPD Sozialdemokratische Partei Deutschlands / Social Democratic Party of Germany (West German)

SPK Staatliche Plankommission / State Planning Commission (East German)

Stasi Staatssicherheit / Ministry for State Security (East German)

StGB Strafgesetzbuch / criminal code

SU Sowjetunion / Soviet Union

UN United Nations

USA United States of America

USSR Union of Soviet Socialist Republics

VEB Volkseigener Betrieb / state owned enterprise

Vopo Volkspolizei / Volkspolizist / People's Police / officer (East German)

VP Volkspolizei / People's Police (East German)

VPKA Volkspolizei-Kreisamt / East German police local office

VVS Vertrauliche Verschlußsache / confidential

WDR Westdeutscher Rundfunk / West German broadcasting corporation

ZAIG Zentrale Auswertungs- und Informationsgruppe / Central analysis and information group (Stasi)

ZERV Zentrale Ermittlungsgruppe für Regierungs- und Vereinigungskriminalität / Central Investigation Office for Governmental and Unification Crimes

ZK Zentralkomitee / Central Committee